Uruguay

Anna Maria Espsäter
with Nicolás Kugler

D1354015

Credits

Footprint credits
Editor: Felicity Laughton
Production and layout: Emma Bryers
Maps: Kevin Feeney

Publisher: Patrick Dawson
Advertising: Elizabeth Taylor
Sales and marketing: Kirsty Holmes

Photography credits
Front cover: Joho/Cultura Limited/
Superstock
Back cover: Don Klein/Superstock

Printed in India by Thomson Press (I) Ltd,
Faridabad, Haryana

Every effort has been made to ensure
that the facts in this guidebook are
accurate. However, travellers should
still obtain advice from consulates,
airlines, etc, about travel and visa
requirements before travelling. The
authors and publishers cannot accept
responsibility for any loss, injury or
inconvenience however caused.

Publishing information
Footprint *Focus Uruguay*
2nd edition
© Footprint Handbooks Ltd
August 2014

ISBN: 978 1 909268 72 2
CIP DATA: A catalogue record
for this book is available from
the British Library

® Footprint Handbooks and the
Footprint mark are a registered
trademark of Footprint Handbooks Ltd

Published by Footprint
6 Riverside Court
Lower Bristol Road
Bath BA2 3DZ, UK
T +44 (0)1225 469141
F +44 (0)1225 469461
footprinttravelguides.com

Contents

ARGENTINA

BRAZIL

Bella Unión · *Río Quaraí*
Artigas

Rivera

Termas del Arapey

Salto

Minas de Corrales

Aceguá

Termas de Daymán

Tacuarembó

Termas de Guaviyú ③

Tambores

Ansina

Las Toscas

Melo

Paysandú

Guichón

Curtina

Río Uruguay

Paso de los Toros

Rincón del Bonete (Lago Artificial)

Tres Bocas

Río Negro

Quebrada de los Cuervos

Fray Bentos

Mercedes

Carlos Reyes

Cerro Chato

Soriano

Palmitas ②

Durazno

Sarandí del Yí

Treinta y Tres

Dolores

Trinidad

José R Varela

Nueva Palmira

Cardona

Sarandí Grande

Pirajá

Lascano

Chuy

Calera de las Huérfanas

Nueva Helvecia

Cerro Colorado

Parque Nacional de Santa Teresa

Carmelo

Rosario

San José de Mayo

Florida

Aiguá

Velásquez ⑥

Punta del Diablo

Conchillas

Colonia del Sacramento ④

Colonia Valdense

Canelones

Minas

Castillos

Barra de Valizas

Libertad

Sta Rosa

Solís

San Carlos

Cabo Polonio ⑥

La Pedrera

Río de la Plata

MONTEVIDEO ①

Atlántida

Piriápolis

Maldonado ⑤

La Paloma

José Ignacio

Punta del Este

Atlantic Ocean

N

20 km
20 miles

Uruguay, meaning 'River of the Painted Birds' in Guaraní, is a land of rolling hills, best explored on horseback, or by staying at the many estancias that have opened their doors to visitors. It also has its feet in the Atlantic Ocean and one of the best ways to arrive is by ferry across the shipping lanes of the Río de la Plata. Montevideo, the capital and main port, is refurbishing its historical centre to match the smart seaside neighbourhoods, but its atmosphere is far removed from the cattle ranches of the interior.

West of Montevideo is Colonia del Sacramento, a former smuggling town turned gambling centre, and a little colonial treasure where racehorses take their exercise on the beach. Up the Río Uruguay there are pleasant towns, some with bridges to Argentina, some with thermal hot springs. Also by the river is Fray Bentos, the town that lent its name to corned beef for generations, now home to an industrial museum.

Each summer, millions of holidaymakers flock to Punta del Este, one of the most famous resorts on the continent, but if crowds are not your cup of *mate* (the universal beverage), go out of season. Alternatively, venture up the Atlantic coast towards Brazil for emptier beaches and fishing villages, sea lions, penguins and the occasional old fortress. And anywhere you go, take your binoculars because the birdwatching is excellent.

Planning your trip

Where to go in Uruguay

Montevideo, the capital, is the business heart of the country and has an interesting Ciudad Vieja (old city). The highlights are Mercado del Puerto, the former dockside market, which has become an emporium for traditional food and drink, the magnificently restored Teatro Solís and the pedestrianized Calle Sarandí. Within the city limits are a number of beaches, which continue along the north shore of the Río de la Plata and on to the Atlantic seaboard. The most famous resort is **Punta del Este** which, in season (December to February), is packed with Argentines, Brazilians and locals taking their summer break. Beyond Punta del Este, particularly in the department of Rocha, there are quieter beaches with less infrastructure, but with sand dunes and other natural features. Along the coast, impressive villas and condominiums blend with their surroundings, a sort of museum of contemporary South American architecture under the open sky. Several national parks and nature reserves also line the coast of the eastern parts, towards the Brazilian border, including Santa Teresa and San Miguel, both with impressive fortresses.

West of the capital is **Colonia del Sacramento**, a unique remnant of colonial building in this part of the continent. It is well preserved, standing on a small peninsula, and has one of the principal ferry ports for passenger traffic from Buenos Aires. Consequently it is a popular, if costly place, well worth a visit, as is the nearby historic town of Carmelo. Continuing west you come to the confluence of the Río Uruguay with the Plata estuary. Upriver are the last vestiges of the meat canning industry at **Fray Bentos**, which has a museum commemorating what used to be one of Uruguay's main businesses. Further upstream are towns such as **Paysandú** and the historic **Salto**, from where you can cross to Argentina, and the hot springs which have been developed into resorts.

The centre of the country is mainly agricultural land, used for livestock and crops. Many estancias (farms) accept visitors. Daytrips to an estancia from Montevideo, Punta del Este or Colonia, usually involve a meal, handicraft shopping and an educational element. The ranches that offer lodging let you take part in the daily tasks, as these are working farms; you can do as much or as little as you like. Horse riding is the main activity and is suitable for all. Fishing, hunting and wine tasting are also offered at some. Wine tourism is becoming increasingly popular in Uruguay's three main wine districts and beyond, with wineries offering tours of the vineyards and tastings, and occasionally lodging and culinary experiences as well.

Don't miss...

1 Montevideo's Mercado del Puerto, a vibrant old market building near the harbour, replete with quaint eateries, pages 21 and 28.

2 A stay at one of the many estancias open to visitors; options include everything from the latest in luxury, to authentic rusticity on a working farm, page 33.

3 A dip in one of the many thermal hot springs along Río Uruguay in western Uruguay, pages 40 and 48.

4 Colonia del Sacramento, a colonial gem on Río de la Plata, home to splendid 17th- and 18th-century architecture, page 40.

5 Endless beaches stretching east from Montevideo right up to the Brazilian border, including world-renowned Punta del Este, page 62.

6 National parks on the Atlantic coast, such as Cabo Polonio and Santa Teresa, with stunning sand dunes, isolated beaches and pristine forests, page 69.

Numbers relate to the map on page 4.

Best time to visit Uruguay

The climate is temperate, often windy, with summer heat tempered by Atlantic breezes. Winter (June to September) is damp; temperatures average 10-16°C, but can sometimes fall to freezing. Summer (December to March) temperatures average 21-27°C. There is always some wind and the nights are relatively cool. The rainfall, with prolonged wet periods in July and August, averages about 1200 mm in Montevideo and some 250 mm more in the north, but the amount varies yearly.

Most tourists visit during the summer, which is also high season, when prices rise and hotels and transport need advance bookings. In the low season on the coast many places close, although increasingly they're staying open longer to encourage international and local visitors.

Getting to Uruguay

Air

There are currently no direct flights from the UK to Uruguay, but there are good connections via South American, European or US hubs. Most South American countries have direct flights from Europe. In many cases, though, the choice of departure point is limited to Madrid and one or two other cities (Paris

Driving in Uruguay

Road Driving is very expensive by South American standards: fuel costs are high and many roads have tolls (passenger vehicles US$2.50, payable in UR$, AR$, US$ or reais). Roads are generally in good condition, with a significant proportion paved or all-weather. In rural areas, motorists should drive with their headlights on even in daylight, especially on major roads. Uruguayans are polite drivers: outside Montevideo, trucks will move to let you pass and motorists will alert you of speed traps.

Documents 90-day admission is usually given without any problems. Entry is easier and faster with a *carnet de passages*, but it is not essential. Without it you will be given a temporary import paper which must be surrendered on leaving the country. Insurance is required by law. For more information, see www.aduanas. gub.uy ('Información al Usuario, Trámites y Servicios').

Organizations Automóvil Club del Uruguay, Avenida del Libertador 1532, T1707, www.acu.com.uy. Reciprocity with foreign automobile clubs is available; members do not have to pay for affiliation.

Fuel All gasoline is unleaded: 97 octane, US$2 per litre, 95 octane, US$1.93, *especial* 87 octane, US$1.84 per litre; diesel, US$1.82 per litre. Filling stations may close weekends.

or Amsterdam, for instance). Argentina, Brazil and Venezuela have the most options: France, Germany, Italy, Spain and the UK (although the last named not to Venezuela). Brazil also has flights from Lisbon to a number of cities. Where there are no direct flights, connections can be made in the USA (Miami, or other gateways), Buenos Aires, Rio de Janeiro or São Paulo. Main US gateways are Miami, Houston, Dallas, Atlanta and New York. On the west coast, Los Angeles has flights to several South American cities. If buying airline tickets routed through the USA, check that US taxes are included in the price. Flights from Canada are mostly via the USA, although there are direct flights from Toronto to Bogotá and Santiago. Likewise, flights from Australia and New Zealand are best through Los Angeles, except for the Qantas/LAN route from Sydney and Auckland to Santiago, and Qantas' non-stop route SydneySantiago, from where connections can be made. From Japan and from South Africa there are direct flights to Brazil. Within Latin America there is plenty of choice on local carriers and some connections on US or European airlines.

Flight connections If flying from Uruguay to make an international connection in Buenos Aires, make sure your flight goes to **Ezeiza International Airport** (eg **American Airlines** or **Air Europa**), not **Aeroparque** (almost all **Aerolíneas**

Argentinas flights). If you arrive in Aeroparque luggage is not transferred automatically to Ezeiza and you will have to travel one hour between the airports by taxi or bus. If you need a visa to enter Argentina, you must get a transit visa (takes up to four weeks to process in Montevideo), just to transfer between airports. See also Airport tax, page 15.

Prices and discounts

Most airlines offer discounted fares on scheduled flights through agencies who specializing in this type of fare. If you buy discounted air tickets always check the reservation with the airline concerned to make sure the flight still exists. Also remember the IATA airlines' schedules change in March and October each year, so if you're going to be away a long time it's best to leave return flight coupons open. Peak times are 7 December-15 January and 10 July-10 September. If you intend travelling during those times, book as far ahead as possible. Between February and May and September and November special offers may be available.

Transport in Uruguay

Road

Bus All main cities and towns are served by good bus companies originating from the Tres Cruces Terminal in Montevideo (www.trescruces.com.uy, for schedules and fares, but purchase must be made in person and early if travelling to popular destinations at peak holiday time). There are good services to neighbouring countries. Details are given throughout the book. Most buses are of a high standard and very comfortable, with toilet on board and some even have Wi-Fi. However, more remote locations and smaller towns and villages are served less frequently, particularly after the high season.

Bicycle Cycling is an increasingly popular option and cycle paths are starting to open up, for example around Punta del Este. Uruguay is comparatively flat, making cycling less of a challenge.

Car Driving your own or a rented vehicle (see box, opposite) is a viable way to explore Uruguay, as it allows flexibility and access to further destinations.

Hitchhiking Hitching is not easy.

Train

Passenger services are the slow commuter services from Montevideo. See page 38.

Maps

Automóvil Club del Uruguay (www.acu.com.uy, see box, page 8), publishes road maps of the city and country, as do **Esso** and **Ancap**. **ITMB** of Vancouver also publish a country map (1:800,000). Official maps are issued by **Servicio Geográfico Militar** ① *Av 8 de Octubre 3255, T2487 1810, www.ejercito.mil.uy/cal/sgm*.

Where to stay in Uruguay

There's an increasingly wide range of accommodation in all categories (although slightly fewer mid-range hotels). Luxury accommodation and estancias are particularly good (see box, page 64), but there are also good hostels, many HI affiliated. *Cabañas* and self-catering flats, cottages and houses are good options in high season for families or larger groups. See www.ahru.com.uy and this guide for further information.

Camping

There are lots of sites. Most towns have municipal sites (quality varies). Many sites along the Ruta Interbalnearia, but most of these close off season. The tourist office in Montevideo issues a good guide to campsites and youth hostels; see references throughout the book. See also www.solocampings.com/uruguay.

Youth hostels

Many good-quality hostels can be found in Montevideo and other cities and towns (see recommendations in Where to stay sections). **Hostelling International** ① *Colonia 1086, p9, Of 903, Montevideo, www.hosteluruguay.org*, has 19 member hostels.

Food and drink in Uruguay

Restaurants

Dinner hours are generally 2000-0100. Restaurants usually charge *cubierto* (bread and place setting), costing US$1-3, and more in Punta del Este. Lunch is generally served from 1230-1500, when service often stops until dinner. A *confitería* is an informal place which serves meals at any time, as opposed to a *restaurante*, which serves meals at set times. Uruguay does not as yet have a great selection of international restaurants, although this is slowly changing. Vegetarians may have to stick to salads or pasta, as even the 'meatless dishes' may contain some meat. However, there are a few vegetarian restaurants in Montevideo and, surprisingly, in some of the smaller beach resorts, attracting a more alternative crowd.

Price codes

Where to stay

$$$$ over US$150 $$$ US$66-150
$$ US$30-65 $ under US$30

Price of a double room in high season, including taxes.

Restaurants

$$$ over US$12 $$ US$7-12 $ US$6 and under

Prices for a two-course meal for one person, excluding drinks or service charge.

Food

In most places, you have two choices: meat or Italian food. Beef is eaten at almost all meals. Most restaurants are *parrilladas* (grills) where the main cuts are *asado* (ribs); *pulpa* (no bones), *lomo* (fillet steak) and entrecôte. Steak prices normally indicate the quality of the cut. Also very popular are *chorizos* and *salchichas*, both types of sausage. More exotic Uruguayan favourites include *morcilla* (blood sausage, salty or sweet), *chinchulines* or *chotos* (small or large intestines), *riñones* (kidneys) and *molleja* (sweetbreads). *Cordero* (lamb) and *brochettes* (skewers/kebabs) are also common. Grilled *provolone*, *morrones* (red peppers), *boniatos* (sweet potatos) and *chimichurri* sauce are also omnipresent. *Chivitos* (large, fully loaded steak sandwiches) and *milanesa* (fried breaded chicken or beef) are also popular; usually eaten with mixed salad (lettuce, tomato, onion) or chips. All Italian dishes are delicious, from bread and pastas to raviolis and desserts. Pizza is very common and good. Seafood includes squid, mussels, shrimp, salmon, and *lenguado* (sole). For snacks, *medialunas* (croissants) are often filled with ham and/or cheese, either hot or cold; toasted sandwiches and quiches/pies are readily available; frankfurters, known as '*panchos*' are hot dogs; *picada* (crackers or breads, cheese, olives, coldcuts) is a common afternoon favourite. Desserts, mostly of Italian origin, are excellent. *Dulce de leche* (similar to caramel) and *dulce de membrillo* (quince paste) are ubiquitous ingredients. As in Argentina, *alfajores* are a favourite sweet snack. Ice cream is excellent everywhere. High-quality olive oil is produced near Punta del Este; see www.colinasdegarzon.com for tours and tastings. Punta del Este and surroundings also host a food and wine festival in October.

Drink

The beers are good (Patricia has been recommended). Local wines vary, but Tannat is the regional speciality (eg Don Pascual, Pisano) and several bodegas offer tours. See www.bodegasdeluruguay.com.uy and www.uruguaywinetours.com. Whisky is the favourite spirit in Uruguay, normally Johnny Walker. There is also a national brand, Dunbar whisky Uruguayo, a blended whisky that still has a little way to go before reaching international standards, but is worth a sample. The local spirits include *uvita*, *caña* and *grappamiel* (honey liquor). In the Mercado del Puerto, Montevideo, a *medio medio* is half still white wine, half sparkling white (elsewhere a *medio medio* is half *caña* and half whisky). *Espillinar* is a type of Uruguayan rum. Try the *clericó*, a mixture of white wine and fruit juices. Very good fresh fruit juices and mineral water are common. *Mate* is the drink of choice between meal hours. Coffee is good, normally served espresso-style after a meal. Milk, sold in plastic containers, is excellent, skimmed to whole (*descremada* to *entera*).

Essentials A-Z

Accident and emergency

Emergency T911. **Ambulance** T105 or 911. **Medical emergencies** T1727. **Fire service** T104. **Road police** T108. Road information: T1954. Tourist Police in Montevideo, at Colonia 1021, T0800-8226.

Drugs

In Dec 2013, Uruguay became the first country in the world to legalize cannabis/marijuana, as a drug-fighting measure. At the time of writing, the measure did not appear to have had any significant impact on visitors. Bear in mind that crossing borders while in possession of drugs is still a serious offence.

Electricity

220 volts 50 cycles AC. Various plugs used: round 2-pin or flat 2-pin (most common), oblique 2-pin with earth, 3 round pins in a line.

Embassies and consulates

For all Uruguayan embassies and consulates abroad and for all foreign embassies and consulates in Uruguay, see http://embassy.goabroad.com.

Festivals in Uruguay

Public holidays 1 Jan, 6 Jan; Carnival; Easter week (Tourism Week); 19 Apr; 1 and 18 May, 19 Jun; 18 Jul; 25 Aug (the night before is **Noche de la Nostalgia**, when people gather in *boliches* to dance to old songs); 12 Oct; 2 Nov; 25 Dec.

Carnival begins in late Jan/early Feb and lasts for some 40 days until Carnival week, officially Mon and Tue before Ash Wed (many firms close for the whole week). The most prominent elements in Carnival are Candombe, representing the rituals of the African slaves brought to Río de la Plata in colonial times, through drumming and dance. The complex polyrhythms produced by the mass of drummers advancing down the street in the 'Llamadas' parades are very impressive. The other main element is Murga, a form of street theatre with parody, satire, singing and dancing by elaborately made-up and costumed performers.

Business also comes to a standstill during **Holy Week** (or Tourism Week), which coincides with **La Semana Criolla del Prado** (horse-breaking, stunt riding by gauchos, dances and song) Department stores close only from Good Fri. Banks and offices close Thu-Sun. Easter Mon is not a holiday.

Also in Mar/Apr Tacuarembó, in the north, hosts the gaucho festival **Patria Gaucha**. A weekend in Oct is chosen annually for celebrating the **Día del Patrimonio** (Heritage Day) throughout the country: hundreds of buildings, both public or private, including embassies, are open to the public for that day only. Also special train services run.

LGBT travellers

Uruguay has some of the most liberal LGBT laws in Latin America and passed a same-sex marriage law in 2013. There are also anti-discrimination laws and it was the first country in Latin America to allow same-sex couples to adopt children. Although attitudes sometimes lag behind the laws, on the whole, LGBT travellers will face less discrimination here than elsewhere on the continent. For more info about LGBT-friendly places in Uruguay: http://www.friendlymap.com.uy/.

Money → *£1=UR$39.98, US$1=UR$23, €1=UR$31.22 (Jun 2014).*

The currency is the *peso uruguayo*. Bank notes: 20, 50, 100, 200, 500, 1000 and 2000 pesos uruguayos. Coins: 1, 2, 5, 10 and 50 (the latter is rare) pesos. Any amount of currency can be taken in or out. Rates change often.

There's no restriction on foreign exchange transactions (so it is a good place to stock up with US dollar bills, though AmEx and some banks refuse to do this for credit cards; most places charge 3% commission for such transactions).

Dollars cash can be purchased when leaving the country. The rate is usually marginally worse if you change Argentine pesos into Uruguayan pesos. Brazilian reais get a much worse rate. US dollars, Argentine pesos or Brazilian reais notes are accepted for some services, including hotels and restaurants in the main tourist centres.

Most places now have ATMs, including several of the smaller resorts along the coast, but not all. If heading off the beaten track take smaller denomination notes in Uruguayan pesos and US dollars.

Cost of travelling Prices vary considerably between summer and winter in tourist destinations, Punta del Este being one of the most expensive summer resorts in Latin America. In Montevideo, allow US$70-80 daily for a cheap hotel, eating the *menú del día* and travelling by bus. Internet price varies, around US$1 per hr at **Antel** *telecentros*. Away from the main tourist centres you can get away with spending US$50 a day.

Credit cards In some places there is a 10% charge to use Visa and MasterCard. **Banred**, www.banred.com.uy, is the largest ATM network from where you can withdraw US$ or pesos with a Visa or MasterCard. **HSBC, Lloyds TSB, BBVA, Citibank** all have Banred ATMs. **Banco de la República** (BROU) branches have Banred, Link and Cirrus ATMs. ATMs can also be found in supermarkets. Most cheaper hotels outside major cities do not accept credit cards, but this is gradually changing.

Opening hours

Banks: Mon-Fri 1300-1700 (some till 1800). **Businesses**: 0830-1200, 1430-1830 or 1900. **Government offices**: Mon-Fri 1200-1800 (summer); Mon-Fri

1000-1700 (rest of the year). **Shops**: Mon-Fri 1000-1900; Sat 1000-1300; **Shopping malls**: daily 1000-2200. In small towns or non-tourist areas, there is a break for lunch and siesta, between 1300 and 1600.

Postal services

The main post office in Montevideo is at Misiones 1328 y Buenos Aires; open Mon-Fri 0800-1800, Sat and holidays 0800-1300. **Poste restante** at main post office will keep mail for 1 month. Other branches in the capital: on Av Libertador 1440, next to Montevideo Shopping Center, 0800-1300, and under the Intendencia at corner of Av 18 de Julio and Ejido, Mon-Fri 1000-2000, Sat 1700-2200.

Safety

Personal security offers few problems in most of Uruguay. Petty theft does occur in Montevideo, most likely in tourist areas or markets. Beggars are often seen trying to sell small items or simply asking for money. They are not dangerous. The Policía Turística patrol the streets of the capital.

Tax

Airport tax US$19 on all air travellers leaving Uruguay for Buenos Aires, Aeroparque, but US$40 to Ezeiza and all other countries (payable in US$, or local currency), and a tax of 3% on all tickets issued and paid for in Uruguay. Domestic airport tax is US$2.

VAT/IVA 22%, 10% on certain basic items.

Telephone → *Country code +598.*

Ringing: long equal tones, long pauses. Engaged: short tones, short pauses.

In Uruguay, fixed line numbers are 8 digits long. There are no area codes. Mobile phone numbers are prefixed by 9 if calling from outside Uruguay and 09 if calling within the country. **Antel** *telecentros* in cities are good places to find phone, internet and other means of communication.

Time

GMT -3 (Oct-Mar -2).

Tipping

Restaurant and cafés usually include service, but an additional 10% is expected. Porters at the airport: US$1 per piece of luggage. Taxis: 5-10% of fare.

Tourist information

Ministry of Tourism, Rambla 25 de Agosto de 1825 y Yacaré, T2188 5100, www.turismo.gub.uy. For birdwatching, contact: **Avesuruguay/ Gupeca**, Canelones 1198, Montevideo, T2902 8642, www.avesuruguay.org.uy, Mon-Fri 1600-2000. Uruguay is creating a system of national parks under the heading **Sistema Nacional de Areas Protegidas** (SNA), see www.snap.gub.uy (Spanish only).

Useful websites

www.brecha.com.uy *Brecha*,
a progressive weekly listing films,
theatres and concerts in Montevideo
and provinces, US$2 (special editions
sometimes free). Recommended.
www.turismodeluruguay.com
A tourism portal in English, Spanish
and Portuguese.
www.welcomeuruguay.com
Excellent bilingual regional guide to all
tourist related businesses and events.

Visas and immigration

A passport is necessary for entry
except for nationals of most Latin
American countries, who can get in
with national identity documents for
stays of up to 90 days. Nationals of
the following countries need a visa for
a tourist visit of less than 3 months:
China, Egypt, Guyana, Morrocco and
the majority of Caribbean, African,
Middle Eastern, Central Asian and
Asian states. Visas cost US$42, and
you need a passport photo, hotel
reservations or letter of invitation and
a ticket out of Uruguay. Visa processing
may take 2-4 weeks. Visas are valid
for 90 days and usually multiple
entry. Tourist cards (obligatory for all
tourists, obtainable on entry) are valid
for 3 months, extendable for a similar
period at the **Migraciones office**,
C Misiones 1513, T2152 1800, www.
dnm.minterior.gub.uy. If entering
and leaving Uruguay overland (bus
or ferry), you may on departure be
asked to show the ticket with which
you arrived in the country.

Weights and measures

Metric.

Contents

Footprint features

Uruguay

Montevideo

Montevideo, the capital, is a modern city that feels very much like a town. Barrios retain their personality while the city gels into one. The main areas, from west to east, are: the shipping port, downtown, several riverside and central neighbourhoods (Palermo, Punta Carretas, Pocitos), the suburbs and Carrasco International airport, all connected by the Rambla. Everything blends together – architecture, markets, restaurants, stores, malls, stadiums, parks and beaches – and you can find what you need in a short walk.

Montevideo, officially declared a city in 1726, sits on a promontory between the Río de la Plata and an inner bay. Although the early fortifications have been destroyed, Spanish and Italian architecture, French and Art Deco styles can still be seen, especially in Ciudad Vieja. The city not only dominates the country's commerce and culture, it also accounts for 70% of industrial production and handles almost 90% of imports and exports.

In January and February many locals leave for the string of seaside resorts to the east.

Arriving in Montevideo → *Population: 1,340,535 (2012).*

Getting there

Carrasco International Airport is east of the centre, with easy connections by bus or taxi (20-30 minutes to downtown). Many visitors arrive at the **port** by boat from Buenos Aires, or by boat to Colonia and then bus to the **Tres Cruces bus terminal** just north of downtown. Both port and terminal have good facilities and tourist information.

Getting around

The Ciudad Vieja can be explored on foot. From Plaza de la Independencia buses are plentiful along Avenida 18 de Julio, connecting all parts of the city. Taxis are also plentiful, affordable and generally trustworthy, although compact. *Remises* (private driver and car) can be rented by the hour. **Note**: Street names are located on buildings, not street signs. Some plazas and streets are known by two names: for instance, Plaza de la Constitución is also called Plaza Matriz. It's a good idea to point out to a driver the location you want on a map and follow your route as you go. Also, seemingly direct routes rarely exist owing to the many one-way streets and, outside the centre, non-grid layout. ⇥ *See Transport, page 36.*

Tourist information

Tourist information for the whole country is at the **Tres Cruces bus terminal** ① *T2409 7399, trescruces@mintur.gub.uy, Mon-Fri 0800-2200, Sat-Sun 0900-2200*; at the **Ministry of Tourism** ① *Rambla 25 de Agosto de 1825 y Yacaré (next to the port), T21885, ext111*; and at **Carrasco International Airport** ① *T2604 0386, carrasco@mintur.gub.uy, 0800-2000*, which has good maps. For **information on Montevideo**, go to **Mercado del Puerto** ① *Rambla 25 de Agosto de 1825 y Maciel, T2916 1513.* Also at **Piedras and Pérez Castellano 1424** ① *T2916 5287*, **Intendencia de Montevideo** ① *Av 18 de Julio esq Ejido*, at the **airport**, **port** and **Tres Cruces** (see above). Pick up a copy of *Descubrí Montevideo*, a useful city guide with an English version, downloadable from the municipal website, www.montevideo.gub.uy, or www.descubrimontevideo.uy. Check also at the municipal website for weekend tours. See also www.montevideo.com.uy and www.cartelera.com.uy. For the **Tourist Police** ① *Colonia 1021, T0800-8226.*

Maps

The best street maps of Montevideo are at the beginning of the *Guía Telefónica* (both white and yellow page volumes). Free maps are available in all tourist offices and some museums. For downloadable maps go to www.montevideo.gub.uy. *Guía Eureka de Montevideo* is recommended for streets, with index and bus routes (US$8.50-10 from bookshops and newspaper kiosks).

City centre

The oldest square in Montevideo, the **Plaza de la Constitución** or **Matriz**, is in the **Ciudad Vieja**. On one side is the **Catedral** (1790-1804), with the historic **Cabildo** (1804), opposite. It contains the **Museo y Archivo Histórico Municipal** ① *JC Gómez 1362, T2915 9685, Mon-Fri 1200-1745, Sat 1000-1600, free.* The Cabildo has several exhibition halls. On the south side of the square is the **Club Uruguay** (built in 1888), which is worth a look inside. See also the unusual fountain (1881), surrounded by art and antique vendors under the sycamore trees.

West along Calle Rincón is the small **Plaza Zabala**, with a monument to Bruno Mauricio de Zabala, founder of the city. North of this Plaza are: the

Montevideo Ciudad Vieja & Centre

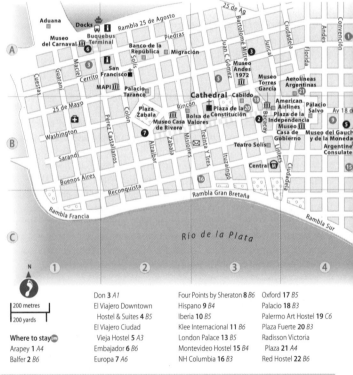

Banco de la República ① *Cerrito y Zabala,* and the **Aduana** ① *Rambla 25 de Agosto*. Several historic houses belong to the Museo Histórico Nacional (see www.mec.gub.uy, or www.museohistorico.gub.uy): **Museo Histórico Nacional (Casa de Rivera)** ① *Rincón 437, T2915 1051, Mon-Fri 1100-1700, free,* is an early 19th-century mansion of the first president of the republic. Its rooms are dedicated to various stages of Uruguayan history. **Palacio Taranco, Museo de Artes Decorativas** ① *25 de Mayo 376, T2915 6060, Mon-Fri 1230-1730, free,* whose garden overlooks Plaza Zabala, is a palatial mansion in turn-of-the-20th-century French style, with sumptuously decorated rooms, and a museum of Islamic and Classical pottery and glass. It was first built as a theatre in 1793 and rebuilt in 1908 after it was bought by the Ortiz de Taranco family. Also in the Ciudad Vieja is the **MAPI (Museo de Arte Precolombino e Indígena)** ① *25 de Mayo 279, T2916 9360, www.mapi.org.uy, Mon-Fri 1130-1730, Sat 1000-1600, US$3,* in a 19th-century mansion, bringing together public and private collections of local and non-Uruguayan artefacts.

Recently opened in a 19th-century building is **Museo Andes 1972** ① *Rincón 619, T2916 9461, www.mandes.uy, Mon-Sat 1000-1700,* a small museum commemorating the 1972 plane crash in which a Uruguayan rugby team survived 72 days in the Andean mountains. Not recommended for children under 12.

The main port is near the Ciudad Vieja, with the docks three blocks north of Plaza Zabala. Three blocks south of the Plaza is the Río de la Plata. Cross the Rambla from the docks to visit the **Mercado del Puerto** (see Restaurants, page 28) and the adjacent **Museo del Carnaval** ① *Rambla 25 de Agosto 1825, T2915 0807, www.museodelcarnaval. org, daily 1100-1700 (closed Tue, Apr-Dec), US$3,* a small exhibition with colourful pictures and costumes from the February celebrations. Proceed south one block to Cerrito, east two blocks to the **Banco de la República** and church of **San Francisco** (1864)

Sur Hotel **23** *C5*

Restaurants 🍴
Bosque Bambú **1** *B5*
Café Bacacay &
  Panini's Boutique **2** *B3*
Corchos **3** *A3*

El Fogón **4** *B5*
Jacinto **7** *B2*
Los Leños Uruguayos **5** *B5*
Mercado del Puerto **6** *A1*
Subte Pizzería **8** *B6*
Tartar **9** *B5*
Viejo Sancho **10** *B6*

① *Solís 1469*, south across Plaza Zabala to Peatonal Sarandí (pedestrianized street) and east to Plaza de la Independencia (see below), stopping at the aforementioned historical sites as desired. Restoration efforts are slow but steady. Although safe by day, with many tourist police, common sense, even avoidance, is recommended at night.

Between the Ciudad Vieja and the new city is the largest of Montevideo's squares, **Plaza de la Independencia**, a short distance east of Plaza de la Constitución. Numerous cafés, shops and boutiques line Peatonal Sarandí. Two small pedestrian zones full of cafés, live music (mostly after 2300) and restaurants, Peatonal Bacacay and Policía Vieja, lead off Sarandí. Below his statue (1923) in the middle of Plaza de la Independencia is the subterranean marble mausoleum of Artigas. Just west of the plaza is **Museo Torres García** ① *Sarandí 683, T2916 2663, www.torresgarcia.org.uy, Mon-Sat 1000-1800, US$3.10, free Wed, bookshop*. It has an exhibition of the paintings of Joaquín Torres García (1874-1949), one of Uruguay's foremost contributors to the modern art movements of the 20th century, and five floors dedicated to temporary exhibitions of contemporary Uruguayan and international artists. At the eastern end of the plaza is the **Palacio Salvo** ① *Plaza Independencia 846-848*, built 1923-1928. The first skyscraper in Uruguay and the tallest South American structure of its time, opinions are divided on its architectural merit. Currently it houses a mixture of businesses and residences. The famous tango, *La Cumparsita*, was written in a former café at its base. On the southern side of the plaza is the **Museo de la Casa de Gobierno** ① *Palacio Estévez, Plaza Independencia 776, Mon-Fri 1000-1700*, with an exhibition of Uruguay's presidential history. Just off the plaza to the west is the splendid **Teatro Solís** (1842-1869) ① *Reconquista y Bartolomé Mitre, T2-1950 3323, www.teatrosolis. org.uy, guided visits on Tue-Sun 1100, 1200, 1600 (Sat also at 1300), Wed free, otherwise US$1 in Spanish (US$2.20 for tours in other languages)*. It has been entirely restored to perfection, with added elevators, access for disabled people, marble flooring and impressive attention to detail. Built as an opera house, Teatro Solís is now used for many cultural events, including ballet, classical music, even tango performances. Check press for listings. Tickets sold daily 1100-1900.

Avenida 18 de Julio runs east from Plaza de la Independencia. The **Museo de Arte Contemporaneo** ① *18 de Julio 965, 2nd floor, T2900 6662, Tue-Sat 1400-2000, free*, holds temporary exhibitions. In the **Museo del Gaucho y de la Moneda** ① *Av 18 de Julio 998, Palacio Heber Jackson, T2900 8764, Mon-Fri 1000-1700, free*, you'll find a survey of Uruguayan currency and a collection of Roman coins, on the one hand, and a fascinating and highly recommended history of the Uruguayan gaucho on the other. Between Julio Herrera and Río Negro is the **Plaza Fabini**, or **del Entrevero**, with a statue of gauchos engaged in battle, the last big piece of work by sculptor José Belloni. Beneath the plaza is the

Centro Municipal de Exposiciones – Subte ① *www.subte.montevideo.gub.uy, Tue-Sun 1200-1900, free,* whoch holds temporary exhibitions of contemporary art, photography, etc. In the **Plaza Cagancha** (or **Plaza Libertad**) is a statue of Peace. The restored **Mercado de la Abundancia** ① *San José 1312,* is an attractive old market with handicrafts, good local restaurants with lunch specials and tango dancing by Joventango three evenings a week. The **Palacio Municipal** (**La Intendencia**) is on the south side of Avenida 18 de Julio, just before it bends north, at the statue of **El Gaucho**. It often has interesting art and photo exhibitions and there is a huge satellite image of the city displayed on the floor of the main hall. The road that forks south from El Gaucho, Constituyente, leads to the beach at Pocitos. The **Museo de Historia del Arte** ① *Ejido 1326, T1950 2191, Tue-Sun 1330-1900, free,* is also in the Palacio Municipal, as is the **Centro de Fotografía** ① *San José 1360, T1950 1219, www. montevideo.gub.uy/fotografia, Mon-Fri 1000-1900, Sat 0930-1430, free,* which has photography exhibitions.

From Plaza Fabini head along Avenida del Libertador Brig General Juan Lavalleja (known as Avenida Libertador), five blocks east of Plaza de la Independencia (buses Nos 173 and 175 from Calle Mercedes) to the immense **Palacio Legislativo** ① *guided visits hourly Mon-Fri 0900-1800 (3 a day in summer), US$3.10,* which was built 1908-1925 from local marble. There are 52 colours of Uruguayan marble in the Salón de los Pasos Perdidos and 12 types of wood in the library. Other rooms are also beautiful. Not far, and dramatically changing the city skyline, is the 160-m-high **Antel building** ① *Paraguay y Guatemala, Aguada, T2928 8517, free guided visits Mon, Wed, Fri 1530-1700; Tue, Thu 1030-1200,* with a public terrace on the 26th floor for panoramic bay views.

Outside the centre

Recently renovated north of the centre, **Mercado Agrícola de Montevideo** (**MAM**) ① *José L Terra 2220, T2200 9535, www.mam.com.uy, daily 0900-2200,* has a longstanding history as a market place. Housed in a 19th-century building, this is more than just your average farmers' market. Apart from the numerous stalls, there are events, a museum and a theatre on the premises, as well as plenty of food options. Art enthusiasts should head for the **Espacio de Arte Contemporáneo** (**EAC**) ① *Arenal Grande 1930, T2929 2066, www. eac.gub.uy, Wed-Sat 1400-2000, Sun 1100-1700, free, guided visits Sat 1700, Sun 1200,* a few blocks west of Tres Cruces terminal. EAC is housed inside the old Miguelete prison, which makes for a somewhat surreal art experience. It houses permanent and temporary art exhibitions. The **Centro Cultural y Museo de la Memoria** ① *Av de las Instrucciones 1057, Prado, T2355 5891, http:// museodelamemoria-montevideo.blogspot.co.uk/, Mon-Sat 1300-1900, free,* is a fascinating space depicting the horrors of Uruguay's 1970s-80s dictatorship. The **Museo Municipal de Bellas Artes Juan Manuel Blanes** ① *Millán 4015,*

Prado, T2336 2248, http://blanes.montevideo.gub.uy/, Tue-Sun 1215-1745, free, in the ex-Quinta Raffo (a late 19th-century mansion), is dedicated to the work of the artist Blanes (1830-1901). It also displays the work of other Uruguayan artists, including has a room of the works of Pedro Figari (1861-1938), a lawyer who painted strange, naive pictures of peasant life and ceremonies of the Afro-Uruguayans. To get there, take buses No 148 or 149 from Mercedes. The **Museo Zoológico** ① *Rambla República de Chile 4215, Buceo, T2622 0258, Tue-Sat 1015-1545, free,* is well displayed and arranged, and is great for children. To get there, take bus No 104 from 18 de Julio, although it was closed for refurbishment at the time of writing; check at tourist information for reopening details.

In the **Puerto del Buceo**, following the coast eastwards away from the centre, the ship's bell of *HMS Ajax* and rangefinder of the German pocket-battleship, *Graf Spee*, can be seen at the **Naval Museum** ① *Rambla Charles de Gaulle y Luis A de Herrera, Buceo, T2622 1084, 0800-1200, 1400-1800, closed Thu, free.* Both ships were involved in the Battle of the River Plate (13 December 1939), after which *Graf Spee* was scuttled off Montevideo. The museum also has displays of documentation from this battle, naval history from the War of Independence onwards and on the sailing ship *Capitán Miranda*, which circumnavigated the globe in 1937-1938.

Parque Batlle y Ordóñez (reached eastwards of Avenida 18 de Julio), has numerous statues: the most interesting group is the well-known **La Carreta** monument, by José Belloni, showing three yoke of oxen drawing a wagon. In the grounds is the **Estadio Centenario**, the national 65,000-seater football stadium and a football museum, an athletics field and a bicycle race-track (bus No 107). The first football World Cup was held in Centenario Stadium in 1930 and was won by Uruguay. The **Planetarium** ① *next to the Jardín Zoológico, at Av Rivera 3275, T2622 9109, free,* gives good, 40-minute shows on Saturday and Sunday (also Tuesday-Friday on holidays). To get there, take bus 60 from Avenida 18 de Julio, or buses No 141, 142 or 144 from San José.

From the Palacio Legislativo, Avenida Agraciada runs northwest to **Parque Prado**, the oldest of the city's many parks, about 5 km from Avenida 18 de Julio (bus No 125 and others). Among fine lawns, trees and lakes is a rose garden planted with 850 varieties and the monument of **La Diligencia** (the stage coach). Part of the park is the adjacent **Jardín Botánico** ① *daily summer 0700-1800, winter 0700-1700, guided tours, T2336 4005.* It is reached via Avenida 19 de Abril (bus No 522 from Ejido next to Palacio Municipal), or via Av Dr LA de Herrera (bus 147 from Paysandú). The most popular park is **Parque Rodó**, on Rambla Presidente Wilson, with an open-air theatre, an amusement park, and a boating lake. At the eastern end is the **Museo Nacional de Artes Visuales** ① *Tomás Giribaldi 2283 esq Herrera y Reissig, T2711 6054, www.mnav.gub.uy, Tue-Sun 1400-1700, free,* a collection of contemporary plastic arts, plus a room devoted to Juan Manuel Blanes. Recommended.

Within the city limits, the **Punta Carretas**, **Pocitos** and **Buceo** neighbourhoods are the nicest, with a mix of classical homes, tall condos, wonderful stores, services, restaurants, active beaches, parks, and two major malls: The **Montevideo Shopping Center** ① *Herrera 1290 y Laguna, 1 block south of Rivera, www.montevideoshopping.com.uy*, on the east edge of Pocitos, and **Punta Carretas Shopping** ① *Ellauri 350, www.puntacarretasweb. com.uy*, close to Playa Pocitos in the former prison. Outside the city along Rambla Sur, the affluent **Carrasco** suburb has large homes, quieter beaches, parks and services. **Parque Roosevelt**, a green belt stretching north, and the international airport are nearby. The express bus D1 (US$1.40) runs to Carrasco every 20 minutes Monday to Saturday (about every hour Sunday and holidays) along Avenida 18 de Julio and the Rambla and is about 30 minutes quicker, and more comfortable than ordinary buses.

At the western end of the bay is the **Cerro**, a 139-m-high hill (from which Montevideo gets its name), with the Fortaleza General Artigas, an old fort, at the top. It is now the **Museo Militar** ① *T2313 6716, Wed-Sun 1000-1700, free (fort visit US$0.90)*, and houses historical mementos, documentation of the War of Independence and has one of the only panoramic views of Montevideo. The Cerro is surmounted by the oldest lighthouse in the country (1804). To get there, take a bus No 125 'Cerro' from Mercedes.

Bathing **beaches** stretch along Montevideo's waterfront, from Playa Ramírez in the west to Playa Carrasco in the east. The waterfront boulevard, **Rambla Naciones Unidas**, is named along its several stretches in honour of various nations. Bus No 104 from Aduana, which goes along Avenida 18 de Julio, gives a pleasant ride past Pocitos, Punta Gorda and all the beaches to Playa Miramar, beyond Carrasco; the total journey time from Pocitos to Carrasco, 35 minutes (the bus route is further inland in winter). The seawater, despite its muddy colour (sediment stirred up by the Río de la Plata), is safe to bathe in and the beaches are clean. Lifeguards are on duty during the summer months.

ⓘMontevideo listings

For hotel and restaurant price codes and other relevant information, see pages 10-12.

🛏 Where to stay

Non-residents are exempt from paying 22% IVA (VAT), which is usually listed separately in upper category hotels, but may be included in cheaper and mid-range options; check when booking. High season is 15 Dec-15 Mar, book ahead; many beach hotels only offer full board during this time. After 1 Apr prices are reduced and some hotel dining rooms shut down. During Carnival, prices go up by 20%. The city is visited by Argentines at weekends, when many hotels increase prices. Midweek prices may be lower than those posted.

The tourist office has information on the more expensive hotels. **Holiday Inn**, www.holidayinn.com.uy, **Ibis**, www.ibis.com, and others, are represented. For more information and reservations contact **Asociación de Hoteles y Restaurantes del Uruguay**, Gutiérrez Ruiz 1215, T2908 0141, www.ahru.com.uy. All those listed below have been recommended.

City centre *p20, map p20*
$$$$ Don, Piedras 234, T2915 9999, www.donhotel.com.uy. Boutique hotel in 1930s building opposite Mercado del Puerto. With breakfast, 3 standards of room, all modern services including safe in room, restaurant.
$$$$ Four Points by Sheraton, Ejido 1275, T2901 7000, www.four pointsmontevideo.com. Stylish hotel in the heart of Montevideo with all the mod cons. Indoor pool on the 10th floor, overlooking the city, spa treatments, cosy bar and fine dining.
$$$$ Radisson Victoria Plaza, Plaza Independencia 759, T2902 0111, www.radisson.com/montevideouy. Excellent restaurant (rooftop, fine views, Mon-Fri, lunchtime only), less formal restaurant in lobby, luxurious casino in basement, with new 5-star wing, art and antiques gallery, business centre (for guests only), pool, spa.
$$$ Balfer, Z Michelini 1328, T2902 0073, www.hotelbalfer.com. Good, safe deposit, excellent breakfast.
$$$ El Viajero Downtown Hostel and Suites, Soriano 1073, T2908 2913, www.elviajerohostels.com.

Private en suite with a/c and TV, dorms en suite (**$**), breakfast included, barbecue area, bar, outdoor terrace, free Wi-Fi, bike rental.
$$$ Embajador, San José 1212, T2902 0012, www.hotelembajador. com. Sauna, swimming pool in the summer, parking, medical services, free computer use, excellent all round.
$$$ Europa, Colonia 1341, T2902 0045, www.hoteleuropa.com.uy. Comfortable, spacious rooms, good choice in this price range, buffet breakfast, restaurant, parking.
$$$ Hispano, Convención 1317, T2900 3816, www.hispanohotel.com. Comfortable with good services, laundry, parking.
$$$ Klee Internacional, San José 1303, T2902 0606, www.klee.com.uy. Very comfortable, good value in standard rooms, spacious, buffet breakfast, heater, minibar, good view.
$$$ London Palace, Río Negro 1278, T2902 0024, www.lphotel.com. Well established, convenient, excellent breakfast, parking. Associated with restaurant **El Fogón** (see page 28).
$$$ NH Columbia, Rambla Gran Bretaña 473, T2916 0001, www.nh-hotels.com. 1st class, overlooking the river in Ciudad Vieja. Well-appointed rooms, restaurant, sauna, fitness room.
$$$ Oxford, Paraguay 1286, T2902 0046, www.hoteloxford.com.uy. Good buffet breakfast, safes, laundry service, parking.
$$$ Plaza Fuerte, Bartolomé Mitre 1361, T2915 6651, www.plazafuerte. com. Restored 1913 building, historical monument, safe, restaurant, pub.

$$$-$$ Iberia, Maldonado 1097,
T2901 3633, www.internet.com.uy/
hoiberia. Very helpful staff, bike rental,
stereos, minibar. US$6 for breakfast.
Modern and refurbished.

$$$-$$ Sur Hotel, Maldonado 1098,
T2908 2025, www.surhotel.com.
Colourful, refurbished, welcoming,
some rooms with balconies. Good
continental breakfast for US$5, 24-hr
room service, jacuzzi in 2 rooms.

$$ Arapey, Av Uruguay 925, near
Convención, T2900 7032, www.arapey.
com.uy. Slightly run-down old building,
in central location. Variety of rooms
with fan, heating, no breakfast. Wi-Fi.

$$ El Viajero Ciudad Vieja Hostel,
Ituzaingó 1436, T2915 6192, www.
ciudadviejahostel.com. HI affiliate,
hostel with lots of services (Spanish
and tango lessons, bike hire, city tours,
laundry, theatre tickets, football),
double rooms and shared bedrooms
(**$**), safes, airport transport, helpful staff.

$$ Palacio, Bartolomé Mitre 1364,
T2916 3612, www.hotelpalacio.
com.uy. Old hotel, a bit run down,
superior rooms with balconies, laundry
service, stores luggage, no breakfast,
frequently booked, good value.

$$-$ Red Hostel, San José 1406,
T2908 8514, www.redhostel.com.
By the Intendencia, hostel with dorms
and 1 double, all with shared bath,
cheerful, computers, safe, breakfast, roof
terrace and kitchen. Closed at the time
of writing, but re-opening Dec 2014.

$ pp Montevideo Hostel, Canelones
935, T2908 1324, www.montevideo
hostel.com.uy. HI affiliate. Open all year,
24 hrs (seasonal variations), dormitory
style, kitchen, breakfast included,

can be noisy in street-facing rooms,
bicycle hire US$6.60 all day. Family-run,
friendly and recommended.

Outside the centre *p23*
Tres Cruces, Palermo

$$$ Days Inn, Acevedo Díaz 1821,
T2400 4840, www.daysinn.com.uy.
Buffet breakfast, safe, coffee shop and
health club, look for promotional offers.

$$$ Tres Cruces, Miguelete 2356
esq Acevedo Díaz, T2402 3474,
www.hoteltrescruces.com.uy.
Safe, café, decent buffet breakfast.
Disabled access.

$$$-$$ Palermo Art Hostel,
Gaboto 1010, T2410 6519, www.
palermoarthostel.com. Cosy and
colourful, bar and live music, private
and shared rooms (**$**), pool, terrace,
bike rental, near beach and US
Embassy, a good choice.

**$$-$ Unplugged Hostel Suites
Centro**, Colonia 2063, T2401 5787,
www.unpluggedhostel.com. Laid-back
hostel with private rooms and dorms
on 5 floors near Tres Cruces bus
station. Also has a branch in Pocitos
and another in Punta del Diablo (see
page 78).

East of the centre (Punta Carretas, Pocitos)

$$$$-$$$ Ermitage, Juan Benito
Blanco 783, T2710 4021, www.
ermitagemontevideo.com. Near Pocitos
beach, remodelled 1945 building,
rooms, apartments and suites, some
with great views, buffet breakfast.

$$$$-$$$ Pocitos Plaza, Juan Benito
Blanco 640, Pocitos, T2712 3939,
www.pocitosplazahotel.com.uy.

Modern building in pleasant residential district, next to the river, with large functional rooms, buffet breakfast, gym and sauna.

$ pp Pocitos Hostel, Av Sarmiento 2641 y Aguilar, T2711 8780, www. pocitos-hostel.com. Rooms for 2 to 6 (mixed and women only), use of kitchen, *parrilla*, towels extra (US$2), Spanish classes.

Carrasco

$$$$ Belmont House, Av Rivera 6512, T2600 0430, www.belmont house.com.uy. 5-star, 28 beautifully furnished rooms, top quality, excellent restaurant **Allegro**, pub/bar **Memories**, English tearoom 1700-2000, pool, 3 blocks from beach.

$$$$ Cottage, Miraflores 1360, T2600 1111, www.hotelcottage.com.uy. In a prime location next to wide beaches and in quiet residential surroundings, very comfortable, simply furnished rooms with minibar, restaurant **Rambla**, bar 1940, pool in a lovely garden, excellent.

$$$$ Regency Suites, Gabriel Otero 6428, T2600 1383, www.regencysuites. com.uy. Good boutique-style hotel with all services, fitness centre, pool, restaurant **Cava** and pub/wine bar, a couple of blocks from the beach. In same group and price range is the contemporary **Regency Rambla**, República de México 6079, T2601 5555, www.regencyrambla.com.uy.

$$$$ Sofitel Montevideo Casino & Spa Carrasco, Rambla México 6451, T2604 6060, www.sofitel.com. This 100-year-old hotel and casino has been beautifully restored over a period of 3 years and offers 93 rooms and 23 suites on the Carrasco waterfront. State-of-the-art relaxing **So Spa**, fantastic bar and excellent restaurant. Recommended.

❼ Restaurants

There is a 22% tax on restaurant bills that is usually included, plus a charge for bread and service (*cubierto*) that varies between US$1-3 per person.

City centre *p20, map p20*
$$$ Café Bacacay, Bacacay 1306 y Buenos Aires, T2916 6074, www. bacacay.com.uy. Closed Sun. Good music and atmosphere, food served, try the specials.

$$$ Corchos, 25 de Mayo 651, T2917 2051, www.corchos.com.uy. Mon-Fri 1100-1700, also Fri night 2000-2400. Bistro, wine bar and wine shop, 3 different lunchtime set menus from US$10, specializes in Uruguayan wines and gourmet dishes to accompany them.

$$$ Crocus, San Salvador y Minas (Palermo), T2411 0039. Closed Sun. Excellent meals with French and Mediterranean touches.

$$$ El Fogón, San José 1080. Open 1200-0000. Good value typical food, always full, arrive by 2000.

$$$ El Mercado del Puerto, opposite the Aduana, C Piedras, between Maciel and Pérez Castellanos (take 'Aduana' bus), www.mercadodelpuerto.com.uy. Don't miss eating at this 19th-century market building. Choose from delicious grills cooked on huge charcoal grates or more international fare like Spanish tapas and pasta. Best to go at lunchtime, especially Sat; the atmosphere's great, open until 1800 (last orders 1700). Inside the Mercado del Puerto, those recommended are: **Roldós**, sandwiches, most people start with a *medio medio* (half still, half sparkling white wine). **El Palenque**, famed as the finest restaurant, try their excellent *clericó*. **La Estancia del Puerto**, **Cabaña Verónica** and **La Chacra del Puerto**. By far the busiest at lunchtime any day of the week is **Empanadas Carolina** with over 20 varieties to choose from.

$$$ Jacinto, Sarandí 349, T2915 2731. Well-known chef Lucía Soria runs this pleasant, light and airy restaurant in the old town. Good lunchtime *menú del día*, pastas, Uruguayan wines.

$$$ Los Leños Uruguayos, San José 909, T2900 2285. www.parrilla.com.uy. Good and smart *parrilla*, with an extensive and varied menu, including rice and pasta dishes, fish and seafood.

$$$ Panini's Boutique & Deli, Bacacay 1341 (also at 26 de Marzo 3586, Pocitos). Deli and lunchtime café. Good salads and meal deals.

$$$ Viejo Sancho, San José 1229. Closed Sun. Excellent, popular with locals; set menus for US$12.50 per person. Recommended.

$$ Bosque Bambú, San José 1060, Asian, vegan and vegetarian buffet, eat in or take away. Also food shop.

$$ Subte Pizzería, Ejido 1327, T2902 3050. An institution, cheap and good.

$ Tartar, San José 1096, T2902 3154. Tiny café selling fresh fruit juices, *empanadas*, savoury pies and *chivitos*. Lunchtime specials US$4.50.

Outside the centre *p23*
In and around Pocitos

$$$ Bar Tabaré, Zorrilla de San Martín 152/54, T2712 3242. Wonderful restaurant in a converted old *almacén* (grocery shop). Great wines and entrées.

$$$ Da Pentella, Luis de la Torre 598, esq Francisco Ros, T2712 0981. Amazing Italian and seafood, artistic ambience, great wines.

$$$ El Viejo y el Mar, Rambla Gandhi 400 y Solano García, Punta Carretas, T2710 5704. Fishing community atmosphere with a great location by the river.

$$$ Francis, Luis de la Torre 502, Punta Carretas (also has a branch in Carrasco at Av Arocena 1692), T2711 8603, www.francis.com.uy. Wonderfully versatile restaurant with a great selection of sushi, salads and rice dishes, as well as gourmet *parrilla* and seafood.

$$$ Gardenia, World Trade Center Plaza, local 052, Av LA de Herrera 1248, T2628 8838, www.gardeniamvd. com. Elegant restaurant, fine dining, cocktails and winelist.

$$$ La Otra, Tomás Diago 752 y Juan Pérez, T2711 3006. Specializes in meat, lively.

$$$ Spaghetteria 32, Franzini y Carlos Berg, T2710 9769. Closed Mon. Very good Italian choice, serving excellent home-made pasta.

$$$-$$ La Perdiz, Guipúzcoa 350, Punta Carretas, T2711 8963, www. restaurantlapedriz.com. Lively *parrillada* with excellent service. Plenty of freshly grilled seafood and meats. Popular.

\$\$ Pizzería Trouville, 21 de Septiembre y Francisco Vidal (also at Pereira y 26 de Marzo). A traditional pizza place with tables outside, next to the beach.

\$\$ Tranquilo Bar, 21 de Septiembre 3104. Very popular restaurant/bar, great lunch menu.

Carrasco/Punta Gorda

Several restaurants on Av Arocena close to the beach, packed Sun midday.

\$\$\$ Café Misterio, Costa Rica 1700, esq Av Rivera, T2601 8765. Lots of choice on menu, sushi, cocktails. Completely new decor and menu every 6 months.

\$\$\$ García, Arocena 1587, T2600 2703. Spacious, indoor and outdoor seating, large wine selection, rack of lamb is a speciality.

\$\$\$ Hemingway, Rambla México 5535, on west side of Punta Gorda, T2600 0121. Decent food, worth going for amazing sunset views of river and city, great outdoor seating.

Confiterías Café Brasilero, Ituzaingó 1447, half a block from Plaza Matriz towards the port. Small entrance; easy to miss. A must, one of the oldest cafés in Montevideo and a permanent hangout of one of the greatest Latin American writers, Eduardo Galeano. Others include: **Amaretto**, 21 de Septiembre y Roque Graseras, Punta Carretas. Excellent Italian coffee and pastries. **Bar Iberia**, Uruguay esq Florida. Locals' bar. **Phliomene Café**, Solano García 2455, Punta Carretas, www.philomenecafe.com. Parisian-style café. **Manchester Bar**, 18 de Julio 899. Good for breakfasts. **Oro del Rhin**, Convención 1403 (also at Pocitos riverfront, on Plaza Cagancha and at shopping malls). Mon-Fri 0830-2000 (Sat till 1400), open since 1927 it retains the feel of an elegant *confitería* serving good cakes and sandwiches or vegetable pies for lunch.

Options with multiple locations

Several good restaurants and establishments have locations in many neighbourhoods and serve typical Uruguayan fare. Among these are family restaurants: **La Pasiva**, **Don Pepperone** and **Il Mondo della Pizza**. A popular bakery chain is **Medialunas Calentitas**, great for coffee and croissants. 2 popular *heladerías* (ice cream parlours) are **La Cigale** and **Las Delicias**.

☉ Bars and clubs

City centre *p20, map p20*
For **boliches** head to **Sarandí**, **Bacacay** or **Bartolomé Mitre** in Ciudad Vieja, or to **Pocitos** and **Punta Carretas**. Discos charge US\$5-10. Bars/discos/pubs offering typical local nightlife include:

503 Bar, Aguilar 832, just north of Ellauri. Open all day 1930-0400. Pool tables, only steel tip dart bar in town, small wood frame entrance, no sign.

Baar Fun-Fun, Ciudadela 1229, Ciudad Vieja, T2915 8005, www.barfunfun.com. Hangout of local artists, founded in 1895, used to be frequented by Carlos Gardel, where *uvita*, the drink, was born. Great music Fri and Sat. Recommended.

El Lobizón, Zelmar Michelini 1264, www.ellobizon.com. Popular restaurant open till very late with rock and fusion live performances.
El Pony Pisador, Bartolomé Mitre 1326, Ciudad Vieja. Popular with the young crowd. Live music. Also at LA de Herrera e Iturriaga, Pocitos.
La Ronda, Ciudadela 1182 y Canelones. Closed Sun, Mon. Drinks, good food, interesting music and events, with **Cheesecake Records** next door (see Facebook).
The Shannon Irish pub, Bartolomé Mitre 1318, www.theshannon.com.uy. Pub with almost daily live shows and DJs on Thu.
Viejo Mitre, Bartolomé Mitre 1321, Ciudad Vieja. Open till late all week. Mixed music, outside tables.

Outside the centre *p23*
Parque Rodó and around
Asia de Cuba, World Trade Center, Torre 3, local 051, LA de Herrera 1248, T2628 6102, www.asisdecuba.com.uy. Elegant club housed inside the World Trade Center, trendy crowd, good cocktails.
Living, Paullier y Hugo Prato (tuliving on Facebook). Wed-Sun 2100-0500. Popular corner bar.
El Mingus, San Salvador 1952 esq Jackson, T2410 9342, www.elmingus. com. Jazz and blues, home-made food, drinks, great atmosphere.
'W' Lounge, Rambla Wilson y Requena García. Fri-Sat 2300, live music on Sat. Fashionable place for young people, rock, electronica, Latin.

⊙ Entertainment

Montevideo *p18, map p20*
Cinema
See http://cultura.montevideo.gub.uy for listings. Blockbusters often appear soon after release in US, most others arrive weeks or months later. Most films are in English (except non-English and animated features). Modern malls (Montevideo Shopping, Punta Carretas, Portones) house several cine-theatre companies each, including 3D halls. Independent art theatres: **Cine Universitario**, 2 halls: Lumière and Chaplin, Canelones 1280, also for classic and serious films. **Cinemateca** film club, www.cinemateca.org.uy, has 4 cinemas: Cinemateca 18, 18 de Julio 1280, T2900 9056; Sala Cinemateca y Sala Dos, Dr L Carnelli 1311, T2419 5795; and Sala Pocitos, A Chucarro 1036, T2707 4718. The Cinemateca shows great films from all over the world and has an extended archive. It organizes film festivals. Tickets US$6; members US$1 or free.

Tanguerías
El Milongón, Gaboto 1810, T2929 0594, www.elmilongon.com.uy. A show that may include dinner beforehand, Mon-Sat 2100. For tango, milonga, candombe and local folk music. Recommended. **Joventango**, at Mercado de la Abundancia, Aquiles Lanza y San José, T2901 5561, www.joventango.org. Cheap and atmospheric venue, Sun 1930, Mon, Fri and Sun 21.30. **Tango a Cielo Abierto**, Tango Under the Open Sky, in front of Bar Facal, Paseo Yi and 18 de Julio,

T2908 7741 for information. Free and very good Uruguayan tango shows every day at noon on a wooden stage. Highly recommended. **Sala Zitarrosa**, 18 de Julio 1012, T2901 7303, www. salazitarrosa.com.uy is a very popular music venue.
Museo del Vino, Maldonado 1150, www.museodelvino.com.uy. Wine bar and tango show Sat 2200.

Theatres
Montevideo has a vibrant theatre scene. Most performances are only on Fri, Sat and Sun, others also on Thu. Apart from **Teatro Solís** (see page 22), recommended are **Teatro del Centro Carlos E Sheck**, Plaza Cagancha 1168, T2902 8915, and **Teatro Victoria**, Río Negro 1479 y Uruguay, T2901 9971. See listings in the daily press and *La Brecha*. Prices are around US$15; performances are almost exclusively in Spanish starting around 2100 or earlier on Sun. Teatro del Sodre, C Andes esq Mercedes, T2900 7084, www.auditorio.com.uy, home to the national ballet. **Teatro Millington-Drake** at the **Instituto Cultural Anglo-Uruguayo** (known as the 'Anglo'), San José 1426, T2902 3773, www.anglo.edu.uy, puts on occasional productions, as do the theatres of the Alianza Cultural Uruguay-Estados Unidos, Paraguay 1217, T2902 5160, www.alianza.edu. uy (good library), and the Alliance Française, Blv Artigas 1271, T2400-0505, www.alianzafrancesa.edu.uy (concerts, library, excellent bookshop). Many theatres close Jan-Feb.

O Shopping

Montevideo *p18, map p20*
The main commercial street is Av 18 de Julio, although malls elsewhere have captivated most local shoppers. Many international newspapers can be bought on the east side of Plaza Independencia.

Bookshops
The Sun market on Tristán Narvaja and nearby streets is good for second-hand books. Every Dec daily in the evening is **Feria IDEAS +**, a book, photography and crafts fair, at Plaza Florencio Sánchez (Parque Rodó), with readings and concerts (www.ideasmas.com). The selection of English and American books in Montevideo is poor. The following specialize in foreign publications: **Bookshop SRL**, JE Rodó 1671 (at Minas y Constituyente), T2401 1010, www.bookshop.com.uy, also has 12 other branches across Montevideo and in other parts of the country. **Ibana**, International Book and News Agency, Convención 1485 (also Benito Blanco 845). **El Libro Inglés**, Cerrito 483, Ciudad Vieja. **Librería Papacito**, 18 de Julio 1409 and 888, T2908 7250/2900 2872, www.libreriapapacito.com. Good selection of magazines and books, wide range of subjects from celebrity autobiographies to art. **Puro Verso**, Yi 1385, T2901 6429, www. libreriapuroverso.com. Very good selection in Spanish, small second-hand section in English, excellent café,

chess tables. It has another branch on Sarandí 675, **Más Puro Verso**, with good restaurant on 2nd floor.

Galleries

There are many good art galleries. **Galería Latina**, Juan C Gómez 1420, Paseo de la Matriz, T2916 3737, www.galerialatina.com.uy, is one of the best, with its own art publishing house. Several art galleries and shops lie along C Pérez Castellanos, near Mercado del Puerto.

Handicrafts

Suede and leather are good buys. There are several shops and workshops around Plaza Independencia. Amethysts, topazes, agate and quartz are mined and polished in Uruguay and are also good buys. For authentic, fairly priced crafts there is **Mercado de los Artesanos**, www.mercadodelosartesanos.com.uy, on Plaza Cagancha (No 1365), at Espacio Cultural R Barradas, Pérez Castellano 1542, and at Mercado de la Abundancia, San José 1312, T2901 0550, all branches closed Sun. For leather goods, walk around C San José y W Ferreira Aldunate. **Montevideo Leather Factory**, Plaza Independencia 832, www.montevideoleatherfactory. com. Recommended. **Manos del Uruguay**, San José 1111, and at Shopping Centres, www.manos.com. uy. A non-profit organization that sells very good quality, handwoven woollen clothing and a great range of crafts, made by independent craftsmen and women from all over Uruguay.

Markets

Calle Tristán Narvaja (and nearby streets), opposite Facultad de Derecho on 18 de Julio. On Sun, 0800-1400, there is a large, crowded street market here, good for silver and copper, and all sorts of collectibles. **Plaza de la Constitución**, a small Sat morning market and a Sun antique fair are held here. **Villa Biarritz**, on Vásquez Ledesma near Parque Rodó, Punta Carretas. A big market selling fruit, vegetables, clothes and shoes (Tue and Sat early-1600, and Sun in Parque Rodó, 0800-1400).

◑ What to do

Montevideo *p18, map p20*
City tours
Asociación de Guías de Turismo de Montevideo, T2970 0416, www. uruguias.com, runs historical and architecture tours. Check times and availability in English. Tours of the city are organized by the **Municipalidad**, see www.montevideo.gub.uy (go to Paseos) for details.

Estancia tourism
Information on estancias can be found at **Lares** (see below), which represents many estancias and posadas; at the tourist offices in Montevideo; or general travel agencies and those that specialize in this field: **Estancias Gauchas**, Cecilia Regules Viajes, agent for an organization of 280 estancias offering lunch and/or lodging, English, French and Portuguese spoken. Full list of estancias (Establecimientos Rurales) at www.turismo.gub.uy. Ask at these organizations about **horse riding**, too.

Cecilia Regules Viajes, Bacacay 1334, Plaza Independencia, T2916 3012, www.ceciliaregulesviajes.com. Very good, knowledgeable, specialist in estancias, offering a variety of tours in Uruguay, and skiing in Argentina.

Fanáticos Fútbol Tours, Pablo de María 1592 bis, T2986 2325, www.futboltours.com.uy. Tour operator dedicated to Uruguay's national sport. Bilingual tours of several football stadiums, organizes tickets to matches. Free walking tours.

Jetmar, Plaza de la Independencia 725, T2902 0793, www.jetmar.com.uy. A helpful tour operator. Many branches.

JP Santos, Colonia 951, T2902 0300, www.jpsantos.com.uy. Helpful agency.

Lares, Wilson Ferreira Aldunate 1322, T2901 9120, www.larestours.com. Specializes in nature and cultural tours, including birdwatching, wine and gastronomy, art, trekking, horse riding and estancia tourism. Very experienced. Recommended.

Odile Beer Viajes, Plaza Independencia 723 of 102, T2902 3736, www.odiletravel.com. ISO-certified agency offering personalized service in a variety of fields, including sports (marathons, too), city cycling tours, gourmet and wine, bird- and whale watching.

Rumbos, WTC, LA de Herrera 1248 Of 330, T2628 5555, www.rumbos turismo.com. Caters specifically for independent travellers, very helpful.

TransHotel, Acevedo Díaz 1671, T2402 9935, www.transhotel.com.uy. Accommodation, eco-tourism, sightseeing and tailor-made itineraries.

Turisport Ltda, San José 930, T2902 0829, www.turisport.com.uy (also in Pocitos). American Express for travel and mail services, good; sells Amex dollar TCs on Amex card.

Sports

Football (soccer) is the most popular sport. Seeing a game in **Centenario Stadium** is a must, located in Parque Batlle. If possible, attend a game with Uruguay's most popular teams, **Nacional** or **Peñarol**, or an international match. General admission tickets (US$5-15) can be bought outside before kick-off for sections Amsterdam, América, Colombes, Tribuna Olímpica. Crowds in Uruguay are much safer than other countries, but it's best to avoid the *plateas*, the end zones where the rowdiest fans chant and cheer. Sit in Tribuna Olímpica under or opposite the tower, at midfield. **Parque Central**, just north of Tres Cruces, **Nacional**'s home field, is the next best venue. Other stadiums are quieter, safer and also fun. For information try www.ten fieldigital.com.uy, but asking a local is also advisable.

Basketball is increasingly popular; games can be seen at any sports club (**Biguá** or **Trouville**, both in Punta Carretas/Pocitos neighbourhoods). See www.fubb.org.uy for schedules.

Golf: Uruguay has 11 golf courses in total, between Fray Bentos and Punta del Este. Apart from Jan-Feb, Jul-Aug, you should have no problem getting onto the course, see www.aug.com.uy.

Others: Rugby (www.rugbynews.com. uy), volleyball, tennis, cycling, surfing

Wine and tourism

Commercial wine production in Uruguay dates back to the 1870s, when immigrants from southern Europe began growing and making wines in their new homeland. These days, although the wine regions are concentrated in three main areas (the departments of Canelones, Montevideo and San José), vineyards can be found all across Uruguay – only three of its 19 departments have no wine production. Uruguay produces particularly good red wines, the majority made from the Tannat grape, introduced by Basque immigrants. Although it's perfectly possible to sample quality Uruguayan wines in restaurants (in fact most restaurants, even off the beaten track, can usually offer customers local wines), in recent years a large number of vineyards across the country have started to offer wine tours, wine tastings and often also accommodation and gastronomy experiences. Each place offers something slightly different, but all visits tend to include a guided tour and of course a wine tasting. At some, such as **Finca Narbona** (www.narbona.com.uy), near Carmelo (see page 51), it's possible to stay the night and also partake in other activities, while **Juanicó** (www.juanico.com), in Canelones, does birdwatching tours, and at **Garzón** (www.agroland. com), in Maldonado, you can also do an olive oil tasting from their organically grown olives. The **Uruguayan Wine Tourism Association** (www.winesofuruguay. com), founded in 2005, has more information on the vineyards open to the public, as does its sister website **Uruguay Wine Roads** (www.loscaminosdelvino. com.uy), a venture that aims to introduce international visitors to Uruguayan viticulture, founded by Alto de la Ballena winery (www.altodelaballena.com).

(www.olasyvientos.com), windsurfing and kite surfing, lawn bowling, running, and walking are also popular.

Wine tours near Montevideo

For wineries around Montevideo and throughout the country see www. loscaminosdelvino.com.uy. See also box, page 35. Day tours of Punta del Este are run by many travel agents and hotels, US$50-100 with meals.
Bodega Establecimiento Juanicó, Ruta 5, Km 37.5, Juanicó, Montevideo Province, T4335 9735, www.juanico.com.uy.
Bodega Bouza, Camino de la Redención 7658 bis, Montevideo, T2323 7491, www.bodegabouza.com.
Bodegas Carrau, Av Gral Eugenio Garzón 2556, Montevideo, T2320 0238, www.bodegascarrau.com.
The Wine Experience, T9967 5750, http://thewine-experience.com, offers a variety of tours in Montevideo, Colonia, Carmelo and Punta del Este.

⊙ Transport

Montevideo *p18, map p20*
Air

The main airport is at Carrasco, 21 km outside the city, T2604 0329, www. aeropuertodecarrasco.com.uy; 24-hr exchange facilities. If making a hotel reservation, ask them to send a taxi to meet you; it's cheaper than taking an airport taxi. To Montevideo 30 mins by taxi or *remise* (official fares US$42-60, depending on destination in the city, by van US$13 (payable in Uruguayan or Argentine pesos, reais, US$ or euros), T2604 0323, www. taxisaeropuerto.com; about 50 mins by bus. Buses Nos 700, 701, 704, 710 and 711, from Terminal Brum, Río Branco y Galicia, go to the airport US$1.30 (crowded before and after school hours); dark brown 'Copsa' bus terminates at the airport. **COT** buses connect city and airport, US$5.50, and Punta del Este, US$9.

Air services to **Argentina**: for the Puente Aéreo to Buenos Aires, check in at Montevideo airport, pay departure tax and go to immigration to fill in an Argentine entry form before going through Uruguayan immigration. Get your stamp out of Uruguay, surrender the tourist card you received on entry and get your stamp into Argentina. There are no immigration checks on arrival at Aeroparque, Buenos Aires.

Bus

Local City buses are comfortable and convenient, see Sistema de Transporte Metropolitano (STM) pages on www. montevideo.gub.uy and www.cutcsa.

com.uy. A single fare, US$1, may be paid on the bus, otherwise you can buy a rechargeable smart card for multiple journeys at designated places throughout the city. Buses D1 (see Carrasco, page 25), D2, D3, 5, 8, 9, 10 and 11 charge US$1.40. There are many buses to all parts from 18 de Julio; from other parts to the centre or old city, look for those marked 'Aduana'. For Punta Carretas from city centre take bus No 121 from C San José.
Remises: fares from US$32 from airport to city; **Remises Carrasco**, T2606 1412, www.remisescarrasco. com.uy; **Remises Urbana**, T2400 8665.

Long distance During summer holidays buses are often full; it is advisable to book in advance (also for Fri and weekend travel all year round).

Buses within Uruguay: excellent terminal, Tres Cruces, Bulevar Artigas 1825 y Av Italia, T2401 8998 (10-15 mins by bus from the centre, Nos CA1, 64, 180, 187, 188 – in Ciudad Vieja from in front of Teatro Solís); it has a shopping mall, tourist office, internet café, restaurants, left luggage (free for 2 hrs at a time, if you have a ticket for that day, then US$2 up to 4 hrs, 12-24 hrs US$5), post and phone offices, toilets, good medical centre, **Banco de Montevideo** and **Indumex** cambio (accepts MasterCard). Visit www. trescruces.com.uy for bus schedules. Fares and journey times from the capital are given under destinations.

To Argentina (ferries and buses)
You need a passport when buying

international tickets. Direct to **Buenos Aires**: **Buquebus**, at the docks, in old customs hall, Terminal Fluvio-Marítima; Terminal Tres Cruces, Local 28/29, Carrasco airport, Hotel Radisson, and Punta Carretas Shopping, local Miranda; in all cases T130, www. buquebus.com. 1-3 daily, 3 hrs, US$105 tourist class, one way (cheaper if booked online); departure tax included in the price of tickets. At Montevideo dock, go to Preembarque 30 mins before departure, present ticket, then go to Migración for Uruguayan exit and Argentine entry formalities. The terminal is like an airport and the seats on the ferries are airplane seats. On board there is duty-free shopping, video and poor value food and drinks. **Services via Colonia**: bus/ferry and catamaran services by **Buquebus**, from 5 crossings daily from 1 to 3 hrs from Colonia, depending on vessel, fares: US$53 tourist class one way on slower vessel, US$72 tourist class on faster vessel (very good last-minute deals available online in low season). All have 2½-hr bus connection Montevideo-Colonia from Tres Cruces. There are also bus connections to **Punta del Este**, 2 hrs, and La Paloma, 5 hrs, to/from Montevideo. Cars and motorcycles are carried on either route. Schedules and fares can be checked on www.buquebus.com, who also have flights between Uruguay and Argentina. Fares increase in high season, Dec-Jan, when there are more sailings. If you want to break your journey in Colonia, you will have to buy your own bus ticket on another company to complete the trip to/

from Montevideo. **Colonia Express**, at Tres Cruces bus terminal local 31A, T2401 6666, and at the dock in Colonia, www.coloniaexpress.com, makes 2-3 crossings a day between Colonia and Buenos Aires in fast boats (no vehicles) with bus connections to/from Montevideo, Punta del Este and other Uruguayan towns. Fares range from US$18 to US$35 one way, depending on type of service and where bought, or US$45-65 with bus connections to/from Montevideo. **Seacat**, www.seacatcolonia.com, 3 fast ferries to Colonia, 1 hr, US$33-42 one way, with bus to Montevideo US$40-52, and to Punta del Este US$58-66. Offices: Río Negro 1400, at Tres Cruces locales 28/29, T2915 0202, and in Colonia. **Bus de la Carrera** (T2402 1313, www.busdelacarrera. com.uy), **Belgrano** (T2402 8445, www.gralbelgrano.com.ar) **El Cóndor** (T2401 4764) and **Cauvi** (T2401 9196) run road services to Buenos Aires for US$51-59, 7½-8½ hrs.

Services to **Carmelo** and **Tigre** (interesting trip): bus/motor launch service by **Cacciola**, 2 a day, www. cacciolaviajes.com, US$48. Advanced booking is advisable on all services at busy periods. On through buses to Brazil and Argentina, you can expect full luggage checks both by day and night.

To Paraguay, Brazil, Chile If intending to travel through Uruguay to Brazil, do not forget to have Uruguayan entry stamped into your passport when crossing from Argentina. Without it you will not be able to cross the Brazilian border. To **Asunción**, Paraguay, US$142, 22 hrs, Wed, Sat (also Mon in high season) at 1300 with **EGA**, T2402 5165, www.ega. com.uy (and Río Branco 1417, T2902 5335), recommended, meals served, and **Sol de Paraguay**, T2400 3939, Thu, Sun. The through bus route is via Paysandú, Salto, Posadas, Encarnación, to Asunción (there are passport checks at Salto, Posadas and Encarnación). There are very comfortable daily buses to **Porto Alegre** with **EGA** and **TTL** (Tres Cruces local B 27, T2401 1410, www.ttl.com.br), US$87-111, 12 hrs, and **São Paulo** (US$235, 30 hrs, 1 a week each via Florianópolis, US$155, Camboriú, US$165, 20 hrs, and Curitiba, US$187, 23 hrs). Some private tour companies in Montevideo offer excellent deals on overland bus tours to places like Iguazú, Rio de Janeiro, Salvador, Bariloche and Santiago (eg **MTUR Viajes**, www.mturviajes. com.uy, recommended).

Summerbus, T4277 5781, www. summerbus.com, is a new hop-on hop-off, door-to-door backpackers' service, taking travellers from hostel to hostel, with stops in **Montevideo** and all along the coast up to **Punta del Diablo**. Tickets from US$12 can be bought online or at hostels.

Car hire

It is wise to hire a small car (1.3 litre engine) as Uruguay is relatively flat and gas prices are high. A small car can be negotiated for about US$90 per day, free mileage, including insurance and collision damage waiver, if you are hiring a car for at least 3 days (rates are lower out of season). Cheaper weekly rates available. Best to make reservations before arrival. **Autocar**, Mercedes 863, T2908 5153, www. autocar.com.uy. Economical, helpful. **Punta Car**, Cerro Largo 1383, T2900 2772, www.puntacar.com.uy, also at Aeropuerto Carrasco and other locations nationwide. **Snappy**, Andes 1363, T2900 7728, www.snappy.com. uy. **Sudancar**, Av Italia 2665, T2480 3855, www.sudancar.com.uy. Most car companies don't allow their cars to be taken abroad. To travel to Argentina or Brazil, you can use **Maxicar** rentals in Salto, see page 58.

Taxi

The meter starts at about US$0.90 in *fichas*, which determine fares as shown on a table in the taxi. Tipping is not expected but welcomed, usually by rounding up the fare. Do not expect change for large peso notes. Prices go up on Sat, Sun, holidays and late at night.

Train

Uruguayan railways, **AFE**, use outdated trains, but interesting rides for enthusiasts. The old train station has been abandoned, replaced by a nice new terminus next to the Antel skyscraper, known as **Nueva Estación Central** at Paraguay y Nicaragua (Aguada), T2924 8080, www.afe. com.uy. Passenger trains currently only run Mon-Sat only along the 25 de Agosto line. Most commuter trains run north between Montevideo and Progreso (about 5-10 a day), passing some of the country's poorest areas.

Fewer services go beyond Progreso. To Progreso (55 mins, US$1.40), to Canelones (1 hr 20 mins, US$2), to Santa Lucía (1 hr 40 mins, US$2.45), to 25 de Agosto (1 hr 45 mins, US$2.90. Occasionally, long-distance services and a steam-engine run for special events, such as the 48-hr celebration of the Día del Patrimonio (Heritage Day) in Oct. More information, T2924 7328.

❶ Directory

Montevideo *p18, map p20*
Banks Don't trust the few black market money changers offering temptingly good rates. Many are experienced confidence tricksters. Casas de cambio and banks only open 1300-1700 (some till 1800). Airport bank daily 0700-2200. Most banks can be found along 25 de Mayo, Cerrito or Zabala, and on Plaza Matriz, in Ciudad Vieja, and in the centre along Av 18 de Julio. Exchange houses along 18 de Julio, but shop around for best rates (rates for cash are better than for TCs, but both are often better than in banks, and quicker service). **Embassies and consulates** For all foreign embassies and consulates in Montevideo, see http://embassy. goabroad.com. **Internet and telephones** At **Antel** *telecentros*. **Language schools Academia Uruguay**, Juan Carlos Gómez 1408, T2915 2496, www.academiauruguay. com. **Medical services Hospital Británico**, Av Italia 2420, T2487 1020, www.hospitalbritanico.com.uy. Recommended.

Western Uruguay

West of Montevideo, Route 1, part of the Pan-American Highway, heads to the UNESCO World Heritage Site of Colonia del Sacramento and the tranquil town of Carmelo, both increasingly important wine-growing areas. Off the road are the old British mining town of Conchillas and the Jesuit mission at Calera de las Huérfanas. Other roads lead to the Río Uruguay: Route 2 from Rosario to Fray Bentos, and Route 3 via San José de Mayo and Trinidad to the historic towns of Paysandú and Salto. The latter passes farms, man-made lakes and the river itself. There are also many hot spring resorts.

Colonias Valdense and Suiza → *For listings, see pages 49-59.*

Route 1 to Colonia de Sacramento is a four-lane highway. At Km 121 from Montevideo the road passes Colonia Valdense, a colony of Waldensians who still cling to some of the old customs of the Piedmontese Alps. For tourist information, T4558 8412. A road branches off north here to Colonia Suiza, a Swiss settlement also known as **Nueva Helvecia** (population 10,642), with lovely parks, gardens and countryside. In the town is the Santuario de Nuestra Señora de Schönstatt and the first steam mill in Uruguay (1875). The Swiss national day (1 August) is celebrated with great enthusiasm.

The highway skirts **Rosario** (130 km from Montevideo, 50 km before Colonia del Sacramento), which is known as 'the first Uruguayan Museum of Mural Art'. Dozens of impressive murals are dotted around the city, some with bullfights, some with abstract designs.

Colonia del Sacramento → *For listings, see pages 49-59. Population: 26,231. See map, page 42.*

Founded by Portuguese settlers from Brazil in 1680, Colonia del Sacramento was a centre for smuggling British goods across the Río de la Plata into the Spanish colonies during the 18th century. The small historic section juts into the Río de la Plata, while the modern town extends around a bay. It is a lively place with streets lined with plane trees, a pleasant Plaza 25 de Agosto and a grand Intendencia Municipal (Méndez y Avenida General Flores, the main street). The town is kept very trim. The best beach is Playa Ferrando, 1.5 km to the east, easily accessible by foot or hired vehicle. There are regular connections by boat with Buenos Aires and a free port.

Arriving in Colonia del Sacramento

Tourist information Old Gate ① *Manuel Lobo e Ituzaingó, T4522 8506, www.coloniaturismo.com, daily 0800-2000 (0900-1900 in winter)*. The hotel reservations office is at General Flores y Rivera. There's also an information desk at the bus terminal, daily 0900-2000, year-round. **Centro BIT** ① *C Odriozola 434 (next to the port), www.bitcolonia.com*, is a large building complex with an official tourist information centre (daily 0900-2000 (0900-1800 low season), restaurant, terrace, gift shop, lockers, Wi-Fi, toilets, guide booking service and a permanent exhibition on the country and region (show entry US$2.25). Visit www.guiacolonia.com.uy, www.colonianet.com.

All **museums** (www.museos.gub.uy) are open Friday to Monday 1115-1630, closed either Tuesday, Wednesday or Thursday, except the Museo Archivo Regional, which is closed Saturday and Sunday, and the Museo Naval, which closes Monday to Wednesday. Combined tickets US$2.25.

Places in Colonia del Sacramento

The **Barrio Histórico**, with its narrow streets (see Calle de los Suspiros, south of the Plaza Mayor), colonial buildings and reconstructed city walls, is charming because there are few such examples in this part of the continent. It has been declared Patrimonio Cultural de la Humanidad by UNESCO. The old town can be easily seen on foot in a day (wear comfortable shoes on the uneven cobbles), but spend one night there to experience the illuminations by nostalgic replica street lamps. The **Plaza Mayor** is especially picturesque and has parakeets in the palm trees. Grouped around it are the **Museo Municipal**, in a late 18th-century residence, rebuilt in 1835, with displays of indigenous archaeology, historical items, natural history and palaeontology; the 18th-century **Casa Nacarello**, next door, depicting colonial life; the **Casa del Virrey** (in ruins); the **Museo Portugués** (1717) with an exhibition of beautiful old maps; the ruins of the Convento de San Francisco, to which is attached the **Faro** ① *entry US$0.90, daily 1300-sunset, from 1100 at weekends*, a lighthouse from which you can see Buenos Aires on a clear day; and the **Museo Naval** ① *Calle Enríquez de la Peña y San Francisco, T42622 1084*, opened in the historic Casa de Lavalleja in 2009. At the Plaza's eastern end is the **Portón del Campo**, the restored city gate and drawbridge. Just north of the Plaza Mayor is the **Museo Archivo Regional** (1750), a collection of maps, police records 1876-1898 and 19th-century watercolours. The late 17th-century **Iglesia Matriz** ① *C Vasconcellos, beside the Plaza de Armas/Manuel Lobo*, is the oldest church in Uruguay and occasional venue for free concerts. At the end of Calle

Misiones de los Tapes, the tiny **Museo del Azulejo** (1740-1760, rebuilt 1986) houses a collection of Portuguese, French and Catalan tiles, plus the first Uruguayan tile from 1840. At Calles de San José y España, the **Museo Español**

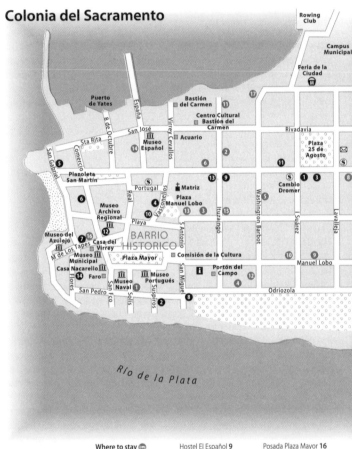

Colonia del Sacramento

200 metres
200 yards

Where to stay 🛏
Charco **1**
Don Antonio Posada **2**
El Capullo Posada **3**
El Viajero B&B **4**
El Viajero Hostel **5**
Esperanza & Artemisa Spa **6**
Hostal de los Poetas **7**
Hostel Colonial **8**

Hostel El Español **9**
Italiano **10**
Posada de la Flor **11**
Posada del Angel **12**
Posada del Gobernador **13**
Posada del Virrey **14**
Posada La Casa de los
Limoneros **19**
Posada Manuel de Lobo **15**

Posada Plaza Mayor **16**
Radisson Hotel,
Casino Colonia &
Restaurant del Carmen **17**
Romi **18**

Restaurants 🍴
Arcoiris **1**
Buen Suspiro **2**

(1720, rebuilt 1840), displays Spanish colonial items plus modern paintings by Uruguayan artist Jorge Páez Vilaró. At the north edge of the Barrio Histórico, the fortifications of the **Bastión del Carmen** can be seen; nearby, in a 19th-century glue and soap factory is the **Centro Cultural Bastión del Carmen** ① *Rivadavia 223*, which hosts frequent theatre productions. In the third week of January, festivities mark the founding of Colonia. The **Feria de la Ciudad** ① *Campus Municipal, Fosalba y Suárez*, is a craft fair worth a visit. Kids will love the **Acuario** ① *Calle Virrey Cevallos 236, esq Rivadavia, www.acuario.com.uy, Wed-Mon 1400-1800, 1600-2000 in summer, US$1.75,* also in the Barrio Histórico.

Around the bay, 5 km away, is **Real de San Carlos**, an unusual, once grand but now sad tourist complex, built by Nicolás Mihanovich 1903-1912. The elegant bullring, in use for just two years, is falling apart and closed to visitors, as bullfighting is now banned in Uruguay. The casino, in those days the nearest to Buenos Aires (where gambling was prohibited), failed when a tax was imposed on Mihanovich's excursions; also disused is the huge Frontón court. Only the **Hipódromo** (**racecourse**) ① *free, except for three annual races*, is still operational, and you can see the horses exercising on the beach. To get to Real de San Carlos, take the 'Cotuc' or 'ABC' bus from Avenida General Flores, leaving Barrio Histórico (US$0.80).

Conchillas

Some 50 km from Colonia and 40 km from Carmelo, Conchillas is a former British mining town from the late 19th century. It preserves dozens

To Real de San Carlos
To ⑦ ⑲
Av Gen Artigas
Cnl Arroyo
Alberto Mendez
Rivera
Dr D Fosalba
V Garcia
To Playa Ferrando (2 km)
⑱
■ Intendencia Municipal
Plaza de Deportes
Av General Flores
To Real de San Carlos
18 de Julio
Av T D Roosevelt
To Montevideo
Centro BIT
PUERTO
To Buenos Aires

Club Colonia **3**
El Drugstore & Viejo Barrio **4**
El Torreón **5**
La Bodeguita **6**
La Casa de Jorge Páez Vilaró **7**
La Florida **8**
Mercosur **9**
Mesón de la Plaza **10**
Parrillada El Portón **11**
Pulpería de los Faroles **12**
Punta Piedra **13**
Tasca del Sur **14**

of buildings constructed by CH Walker and Co Ltd. **Tourist information** is available at the **Casa de la Cultura** ① *C David Evans, daily 0800-1400*. The police station is also a good source of information. Direct buses go to Conchillas from Colonia on the well-marked Route 21.

Carmelo → *For listings, see pages 49-59. Population: 18,041.*

From Colonia, Route 21 heads northwest to Carmelo (77 km) on the banks of Arroyo Las Vacas. A fine avenue of trees leads to the river, crossed by the first swing bridge built 1912. Across the bridge is the Rambla de los Constituyentes and the Fuente de las Tentaciones. The church, museum and archive of El Carmen is on Plaza Artigas (named after the city's founder). In the **Casa de la Cultura Ignacio Barrios (IMC)** ① *19 de Abril 246, T4542 3840*, is a tourist office and museum. Historically a mining centre, it is said that many luxurious buildings in Buenos Aires were made from the grey granite of Cerro Carmelo (mines flooded and used for watersports). It is one of the most important yachting centres on Río de la Plata and its microclimate produces much wine.

Some 10 km before Carmelo, (the exit from Route 21 is clearly marked) **Calera de Las Huérfanas** ① *www.caleradelashuerfanas.org*, also known as Estancia Belén or Estancia de las Vacas, is the remains of one of the area's main Jesuit missions. Vines were introduced and lime was exported for the construction of Buenos Aires. After the expulsion of the Jesuits, its production sustained an orphanage in Buenos Aires. It's in relatively good state and is best reached by car.

Between Carmelo and **Nueva Palmira**, another river port, is the colonial monument, **Capilla de Narbona** (Route 21, Km 263), built in the early 18th century. At **Bodega y Granja Finca Narbona** ① *Ruta 21, Km 268, T4540 4160, www.narbona.com.uy*, see page 51, wine, cheese and other produce are available, as well as a fine restaurant and exclusive hotel rooms.

Mercedes → *For listings, see pages 49-59. Population: 44,826.*

This livestock centre is best reached by Route 2 from the main Colonia–Montevideo highway. Founded in 1788, it is pleasant town on the Río Negro, a yachting and fishing centre during the season. Its charm (it is known as 'the city of flowers') derives from its Spanish-colonial appearance, though it is not as old as the older parts of Colonia. There is an attractive *costanera* (riverside drive) and a jazz festival in January (www.jazzalacalle.com.uy).

Five kilometres west of town is the **Parque y Castillo Barón de Mauá** ① *T4532 2201*, dating from 1857. It has a mansion which contains the **Museum of Palaeontology** ① *T4532 2201 museoberro@gmail.com, daily 1100-1700, free*, on the ground floor. The building is worth wandering around to see the exterior, upper apartments and stable block. Cheese, wine and olive oil are produced. It takes 45 minutes to walk to the park, a pleasant route passing Calera Real on the riverbank, dating back to 1722, the oldest industrial ruins in the country (lime kilns hewn out of the sandstone). Maps and hotel lists are available at the **tourist office** ① *Detomasi 415, T4532 2733, www.sorianoturismo.com.*

Fray Bentos → *For listings, see pages 49-59. Population: 25,047.*

Route 2 continues westwards (34 km) to Fray Bentos, the main port on the east bank of Río Uruguay. Here, in 1865, the Liebig company built its first factory producing meat extract. The original plant, much extended and known as **El Anglo**, has been restored as the **Museo de la Revolución Industrial** ① *T4562 2918/3690, daily 0930-1730, US$2.20 including a 1½-hr guided tour 1000 and 1500 in Spanish (leaflet in English), Tue free.* The office block in the factory has been preserved complete with its original fittings and many machines are on show. Within the complex is the **Barrio Inglés**, where workers were housed, and **La Casa Grande** ① *guided tours Tue, Thu, Sun 1200*, where the director lived. There are **beaches** to the northeast and southwest. **Tourist office** ① *25 de Mayo 3400, T4562 2233, turismo@rionegro.gub.uy, Mon-Fri 0900-1800, Sat 0900-1500.*

Crossing to Argentina
About 9 km upriver from Fray Bentos is the **San Martín International Bridge** (vehicles US$6; pedestrians and cyclists may cross only on vehicles, officials may arrange lifts).

Paysandú → *For listings, see pages 49-59. Population: 78,868.*

North of Fray Bentos, 110 km, is this undulating, historic city on the east bank of the Río Uruguay. Along Route 3, it's 380 km from Montevideo. Summer temperatures can be up to 42°C. There is a 19th-century **basilica** ① *daily 0700-1145, 1600-2100.* The **Museo Histórico Municipal** ① *Zorrilla de San Martín y Leandro Gómez, Tue-Sun 0900-1400*, has good collection of guns and furniture from the time of the Brazilian siege of 1864-1865. The **Museo de la Tradición** ① *Av de los Iracundos, north of town at the Balneario Municipal, daily 0900-1400, Sun also 1800-2100*, exhibiting gaucho articles, is also worth a visit. It can be reached by bus to the Zona Industrial. There is a **tourist office** ① *Plaza Constitución, 18 de Julio 1226, T4722 6220, www.paysandu.gub.uy and www.turismopaysandu.com, Mon-Fri 0900-1900, Sat-Sun 0800-1800 (2000 in summer)*, and another at Plan de la Costa, Balneario Municipal.

Around Paysandú

The **Central Termal Guaviyú** ⓘ *Ruta 3 Km 431.5, T4755 2049, guaviyu@ paysandu.gub.uy, US$3.75-4.50*, are thermal springs 60 km north of Paysandú, with four pools, a restaurant, three motels (**$$$-$$** for 3 to 5 people) and private hotel with its own thermal pools (**$$$**, Villagio). There are also excellent cheap camping facilities. It's a 50-minute bus journey from Paysandú (US$3, six a day). Along Route 90, 83 km east, is the **Centro Termal Almirón** ⓘ *Ruta 90 Km 83, T4740 2873, www.almirontermal.comn@paysandu.gu*, with camping, apartments and motels. The **Meseta de Artigas** ⓘ *free*, 110 km north of Paysandú and 15 km off the highway to Salto (no public transport), is 45 m above the Río Uruguay, which here narrows and at low water forms whirlpools at the rapids of **El Hervidero**. It was used as a base by General Artigas during the struggle for Independence. The terrace has a fine view, but the rapids are not visible from the Meseta. The statue topped by Artigas' head is very original.

Paysandú

Where to stay	Lobato 5	Restaurants
Casagrande 2	Mykonos 6	Artemio 1
El Jardín 3		Los Tres Pinos 2
La Posada 4		

100 metres
100 yards

Crossing to Argentina

The José Artigas international bridge connects with Colón, Argentina (US$6 per car, return), 8 km away. Immigration for both countries is on the Uruguayan side in the same office. If travelling by bus, the driver gets off the bus with everyone's documents and a list of passengers to be checked by immigration officials.

Salto → *For listings, see pages 49-59. Population: 108,197.*

A centre for cultivating and processing oranges and other citrus fruit, Salto is a beautifully kept town 120 km by paved road north of Paysandú. The town's commercial area is on Calle Uruguay, between Plazas Artigas and Treinta y Tres. There are lovely historic streets and walks along the river. See the beautiful **Parque Solari** (northeast of the centre) and the **Parque Harriague** (south of the centre) with an open-air theatre. The **Museo María Irene Olarreaga Gallino de Bellas Artes y Artes Decorativas** ① *Uruguay 1067, T4732 9898, ext 148, Tue-Fri 1600-2100, Sun 1800-2100, free*, in the French-style mansion of a rich *estanciero* (Palacio Gallino), is well worth a visit. **Museo del Hombre y La Tecnología** ① *Brasil 511, T4732 9898, ext 151, daily 1300-1900, free entry and free guided tours in Spanish*, is very interesting, with a small archaeological museum. There is a Shrove Tuesday carnival. The **tourist office** ① *Uruguay 1052, T4733 4096, www. salto.gub.uy, Mon-Sat 0800-1900*, provides a free map; and there's another office at the **international bridge** ① *T4732 8933, salto@mintur.gub.uy*.

The most popular tourist site in the area is the large **Represa de Salto Grande** ① *T4732 6131/7777, rrppmi@saltogrande.org for guided tours 0700-1600 (museum 0700-1500) arranged by Relaciones Públicas office*, a dam and hydroelectric plant 14 km from Salto, built jointly by Argentina and Uruguay. There's a small visitor centre at the plant. A taxi from Salto will cost US$20.50. A road runs along the top of the dam to Argentina. By launch you can get to the **Salto Chico** beach for fishing and camping.

Near the dam (2 km north on ex-Route 3), the 4-ha **Parque Acuático Termas de Salto Grande** ① *T4733 4411, www.hotelhoracioquiroga.com, open all year 1000-1800 (longer Jan and Feb), US$8.50*, has several pools, slides, hydro massages, water jets and a man-made waterfall, all is in a natural setting.

Crossing to Argentina

North of the town, at the Salto Grande dam, there is an international bridge to Concordia, Argentina, open 24 hours a day, all year. Passengers have to get off the bus to go through immigration procedures. Buses don't go on Sundays. Both Argentine and Uruguayan immigration offices are on the Argentine side.

National pride

The indigenous Charrúas were remarkably brave, but they were also inhospitable and rallied against European explorers. They killed Spaniard Juan Díaz de Solís, the navigator who first charted Montevideo in 1515. Between early explorer visits, they learned to ride captured horses, still slinging stones on suede straps in defiance of and indifference to the superior Spanish swords. Their bravery, despite the impossible odds, led to their eradication when the last remaining natives were massacred in 1831. Nevertheless, their legacy lives on. The national soccer team is nicknamed *Los Charrúas* because, after winning the first and fourth FIFA World Cups in 1930 and 1950, against powerhouses Argentina and Brazil, people recognized that 'fight to the finish' attitude in the players. In fact, in Uruguay, it is a great compliment to be described as having *garra charrúa*, meaning strength, resourcefulness, bravery and determination.

Termas del Daymán and other springs → *For listings, see pages 49-59.*

About 10 km south of Salto on Route 3, served by buses marked 'Termas' which leave from Calle Brasil every hour, is Termas del Daymán, a small town built around curative hot springs. It is a nice place to spend a night, though it is crowded in the daytime; few restaurants around the beautifully laid out pools. The **Complejo Médico Hidrotermal Daymán** ① *T4736 9090, www.viatermal. com/spatermaldayman, use of facilities US$4.50, multiple different treatments at additional cost*, has a spa and separate pools (external and internal), showers and jacuzzis. There is also **Acuamania**, a theme park, nearby.

The road to **Termas del Arapey** branches off Route 3 to Bella Unión, at 61 km north of Salto, and then runs 19 km east and then south. Pampa birds, rheas and metre-long lizards are in evidence. Termas del Arapey is on the Arapey river south of Isla Cabellos (Baltasar Brum). The waters at these famous thermal baths contain bicarbonated salts, calcium and magnesium.

To the Brazilian border: Bella Unión

Route 3 goes north to the small town of Bella Unión, from where an international bridge 5 km away crosses to the Brazilian town of Barra de Quaraí. This village lies next to an unspoilt area of densely wooded islands and beautiful sandbanks on the Río Uruguay, at the triple frontier point. About 80 km northwest is **Uruguaiana** which takes the main international bus traffic between Brazil and Argentina.

To the Brazilian border: Artigas

From near Bella Unión Route 30 runs east to Artigas, a frontier town in a cattle raising and agricultural area (excellent swimming upstream from the bridge). The town (population 44,905) is known for its good-quality amethysts. There is a bridge across the Río Cuareim to the Brazilian town of Quaraí. The Brazilian consul is at Lecueder 432, T4772 5414, vcartigas@mre.gov.br.

◉Western Uruguay listings

For hotel and restaurant price codes and other relevant information, see pages 10-12.

◉ Where to stay

Colonia Suiza (Nueva Helvecia)
p40
$$$$ Nirvana, Av Batlle y Ordóñez, T4554 4081, www.hotelnirvana.com. Restaurant (Swiss and traditional cuisine), half- and full-board available, see website for promotions, sports facilities, 25 ha of park and gardens, poolside bar. Recommended.
$$ Del Prado, Av G Imhoff, T4554 4169, www.hoteldelprado.info. Open all year. Huge buffet breakfast, pool, hostel accommodation (**$**).

Tourism farms
$$$$ pp Finca Piedra, Ruta 23, Km 125, Mal Abrigo, northwest of San José de Mayo (convenient for Montevideo or Colonia), T4340 3118, www.fincapiedra.com. Price is full board, various rooms in different parts of this 1930s estancia and vineyard, lots of outdoor activities including riding, tours of the vines, wine tasting, pool, caters for children. Many activities free.

$$$$ La Vigna, T4558 9234, Km 120 Ruta 51 to Playa Fomento, www.lavigna.com.uy. Wonderful boutique eco-hotel, solar-powered and recycled furniture. Offers horse riding and art lessons. Good food, all farm reared and organic. Owner is a cheese-maker, excellent produce. Highly recommended.
$$$ El Galope Farm & Hostel, Cno Concordia, Colonia Suiza, T9910 5985, www.elgalope.com.uy. Access on Route 1, Km 114.5. Discounts for HI members, limited to 10 guests, 6 km from Nueva Helvecia, **$** in bunk bed, use of kitchen, sauna US$10, 2½-hr riding US$35 (beginners US$25 with lesson), bicycles US$1 per hr, walking, English, French, German and Spanish spoken.
$$$ El Terruño, Paraje Minuano, Ruta 1, Km 140, 35 km before Colonia, T4550 6004, www.estanciaelterrunio.com. Price includes breakfast, horse rides and activities.
$$$ pp Estancia Don Miguel, 6 km from Pueblo Cufré, access from Ruta 1, Km 121 y Ruta 52, T4550 2041, www.estanciadonmiguel.com. Rustic, working farm, full board, good activities including massage and reiki, Swedish and English spoken.

Camping

There are several campsites south of Route 1 on Río de la Plata. A good one at Blancarena is **Camping Enrique Davyt** (access from La Paz village east of Colonia Valdense), T4587 2110, campinged@adinet.com.uy, US$3 per person (discount for longer stays).

Colonia del Sacramento *p40, map p42*

Choice is good, including several recently renovated 19th-century posadas.

Barrio Histórico

$$$$ Hotel Charco, San Pedro 116, T4523 5000, www.charcohotel.com. Authentic old town hotel with suites and balcony rooms overlooking the river. Bistro on the premises using vegetables from their own garden.

$$$$-$$$ El Capullo Posada, 18 de Julio 219, T4523 0135, www.elcapullo. com. Spacious living area, English and American owners, stylish boutique-style rooms, outdoor pool and *parrilla*.

$$$$-$$$ Posada Plaza Mayor, Del Comercio 111, T4522 3193, www.posadaplazamayor.com. In a 19th-century house, beautiful internal patio with lemon trees and Spanish fountain, lovely rooms with a/c or heating, English spoken.

Centre

$$$$ Radisson Colonia del Sacramento, Washington Barbot 283, T4523 0460, www.radissoncolonia. com. Great location overlooking the jetty, contemporary architecture, casino attached. 2 pools, jacuzzi,

highly regarded restaurant **Del Carmen**, very good.

$$$$-$$$ Don Antonio Posada, Ituzaingó 232, T4522 5344, www.posadadonantonio.com. 1850 building, buffet breakfast, garden, pool, excellent.

$$$$-$$$ Hotel Esperanza & Artemisa Spa, Gral Flores 237, T4522 2922, www.hotelesperanzaspa.com. Charming, with buffet breakfast, sauna, heated pool and treatments.

$$$ El Viajero B&B, Odriozola 269, T4522 8645, www.elviajerobb.com. Very well located modern building with river views, bike rental.

$$$ El Viajero Hostel Suites Colonia (HI affiliate), Washington Barbot 164, T4522 2683, www.elviajerohostels. com. Private en suite with a/c and TV, dorms en suite with a/c, fireplace for winter, terrace and barbecue area for the summer, breakfast included, free Wi-Fi. Quirky art on walls, recently renovated.

$$$ Italiano, Intendente Suárez 103-105, T4522 7878, www.hotelitaliano. com.uy. Open since 1928, it has been renovated with comfortable rooms, cheaper rates Mon-Thu (low season). Large outdoor and indoor pools, gym, sauna, good restaurant. Recommended.

$$$ Posada del Angel, Washington Barbot 59, T4522 4602, www.posadadelangel.net. Early 20th-century house, pleasant, warm welcome, gym, sauna, pool.

$$$ Posada de la Flor, Ituzaingó 268, T4523 0794, www.posada-delaflor. com. Cheaper Mon-Thu. At the quiet end of C Ituzaingó, next to the river and to the Barrio Histórico, simply decorated rooms on a charming patio and roof terrace with river views.

$$$ Posada del Gobernador, 18 de Julio 205, T4522 2918, www.delgobernador.com. Cheaper Sun-Thu. Charming, with open-air pool, garden.

$$$ Posada del Virrey, España 217, T4522 2223, www.posadadelvirrey.com. Large rooms, some with view over bay (cheaper with small bathroom and no balcony), with buffet breakfast. Recommended.

$$$ Posada Manuel de Lobo, Ituzaingó 160, T4522 2463, www.posadamanueldelobo.com. Built in 1850. Large rooms, huge baths, limited parking, some smaller rooms, nice breakfast area inside and out.

$$$-$$ Romi, Rivera 236, T4523 0456, www.hotelromicolonia.com. 19th-century posada-style downstairs, with lovely tiles at entrance. Airy modernist upstairs and simple rooms. Recommended.

$$ Hostel Colonial, Gral Flores 440, T4523 0347, www.hostelcolonial.com,uy. HI affiliated. Pretty patio and quirky touches, such as barber's chair in reception. **$** in dorm. Kitchen, bar with set meals, free use of bikes (all ancient), run down and noisy, but popular.

$$ Hostel El Español, Manuel Lobo 377, T4523 0759, www.hostelelespaniol.com. Good value, **$** per person with shared bath in dorms, breakfast included, Wi-Fi, TV room. Part of the **HoLa** network of hostels, 10% discount for members. Friendly, recommended.

North of the centre
$$$ Posada La Casa de los Limoneros, Carretera H Mignone y Camino Tomás Assandri, T4523 1028, www.lacasadeloslimoneros.com. 5 rooms in a cute old-fashioned house near lagoon. LGBT-friendly.

$$ Hostal de los Poetas, Mangarelli 677, T4523 1643, www.guiacolonia.com.uy. Some distance from the Barrio Histórico but one of the cheapest, a few simple bedrooms and a lovely breakfast room, tiny exuberant garden. A/c and TV in rooms.

Carmelo *p44*
$$$$ Finca Narbona Granja & Bodega, Ruta 21 km 268, T4540 4160, www.narbona.com.uy. Winery offering accommodation in their wine lodge. Suites overlooking the bodega or the vineyards. Good range of wine-themed activities, including tastings and picnics, as well as biking and horse riding.

$$$$ Four Seasons Carmelo, Ruta 21, Km 262, T4542 9000, www.fourseasons.com/carmelo. 44 bungalows and luxury suites on the shores of Río de la Plata. Golf course, tennis, pools, fine dining and, intriguingly, gaucho-inspired spa treatments.

$$ Timabe, 19 de Abril y Solís, T4542 5401, www.ciudad carmelo.com/timabe. Near the swing bridge, with a/c or fan, dining room, parking, good.

Camping
At Playa Seré, hot showers.

Mercedes *p44*
\$\$\$ Rambla Hotel, Av Asencio 728, T4533 0696. Riverside 3-star hotel with quite good rooms.
\$\$ Ito, Eduardo V Haedo 184, T4532 4919. Basic though decent rooms in an old house.

Tourism farm
\$\$\$\$ pp La Sirena Marinas del Río Negro, Ruta 14, Km 4, T9910 2130/4530 2271, www.lasirena. com.uy. Estancia dating from 1830, picturesque, on the river, birdwatching, fishing, waterskiing, accommodation, meals, full board (**\$\$\$** double room with breakfast) friendly owners Rodney, Lucia and Patricia Bruce. Warmly recommended.

Fray Bentos *p45*
\$\$ Colonial, 25 de Mayo 3293, T4562 2260, www.hotelcolonial.com.uy. Attractive old building with patio. A/c and breakfast extra, **\$** without bath.
\$\$ Plaza, 18 de Julio y 25 de Mayo, T4562 2363, www.plazahotelfray bentos.com.uy. Comfortable, a/c, TV, internet, with breakfast, on the Plaza Constitución.

Camping
Club Remeros, on Rambla Costanera (opposite Parque Roosevelt), T4562 2236.

Paysandú *p45, map p46*
Book hotels in advance during Holy Week.
\$\$\$ Casagrande, Florida 1221, Plaza Constitución, T4722 4994, www.hotelcasagrande.com.uy.

Welcoming, buffet breakfast, restaurant, parking, very good.
\$\$\$ El Jardín, Montevideo 1085, T4722 3745, www.hoteljardin.com. Comfortable family-run residence with private parking, and a neat garden.
\$\$\$ Mykonos, 18 de Julio 768, T4722 0255, www.hotelmykonos.com.uy. Buffet breakfast, mostly a business hotel with good services.
\$\$ Lobato, Leandro Gómez 1415, T4722 2241, hotellobato@adinet. com.uy. With buffet breakfast, modern, good.
\$\$ La Posada, José Pedro Varela 566, T4722 7879, www.hotellaposada. com.uy. Patio with barbecue, buffet breakfast, laundry service.

Tourism farms
\$\$\$\$-\$\$\$ Hostería y Estancia La Paz, Colonia La Paz, 15 km south of Paysandú, T4720 2272, www. estancialapaz.com.uy. Excellent rustic rooms, pool, customized gaucho experiences, horse riding, birdwatching. Half- and full-board available. Highly recommended.
\$\$\$ pp Estancia Resort La Calera, 60 km from Guichón, 150 km east of Paysandú, T2601 0340, www.lacalera. com. 44 rooms, 6 superior rooms and 24 studios, all with fireplace and kitchenette, 2 pools, horse riding and wagon rides, rodeo, sheep shearing, conference facilities. Self-catering. Highly recommended.

Camping
Camping Club de Pescadores, Rambla Costanera Norte, T4722 2885, www.clubdepescadores

paysandu.com. US$3.50 per person per day plus US$6 per tent, electricity, hot showers after 1800.

Salto *p47*
$$$$ Hotel Horacio Quiroga, at Parque del Lago, T4733 4411, www.hotelhoracioquiroga.com. Best in town although some distance from centre, at the Termas complex, sports facilities, spa treatments, staffed by nearby catering school, special packages in season.
$$$ Los Cedros, Uruguay 657, T4733 3984, www.loscedros.com.uy. In centre, comfortable 3-star hotel, buffet breakfast, conference room.
$$ pp Concordia, Uruguay 749, T4733 2735. Oldest hotel in Uruguay, founded 1860, Carlos Gardel stayed here, fine courtyard, pleasant breakfast room.
$$ Español, Brasil 826, T4733 4048, www.hotelespanolsalto.com. Central, functional, with regular services, café and parking.

Termas del Daymán and other springs *p48*
$$$ Hotel Termas del Arapey, T4768 2441, www.hoteltermasdel arapey.com. Safe, indoor/outdoor pool, restaurant, spa, half-board available.
$$$ Termas de San Nicanor, 12 km from Termas de Daymán, Km 485, Route 3, T4730 2209, www. termassannicanor.com. Estancia and gaucho experience, excellent nature watching, private pool. Recommended. Also camping (US$10 per person), good facilities.
$$$-$$ Del Pasaje, near Ruta 3, T4736 9661, www.hoteldelpasaje.com.

Hotel rooms, apartments for 2, 4, 6 or 7 people and *cabañas*. Situated in front of the Parque Acuático Acuamania.
$$ Bungalows El Puente, C 6 y Circunvalación, near the bridge over Río Dayman, T4736 9876, includes discount to thermal baths. 13 bungalows for 2 to 7 people, cheaper without a/c, kitchen.
$$ Estancia La Casona del Daymán, Ruta 3, Km 483, 3 km east of the bridge at Daymán, T4733 2735. Well-preserved farm, horse riding.
$$ Hostal Canela, Los Sauces entre Los Molles y Calle 1, T4736 9121, www.hostalcanela.com.uy. HI affiliated. Good value, with kitchenette, pool, gardens.
$$ pp La Posta del Daymán, Ruta 3, Km 487, T4736 9801, www.laposta deldayman.com. A/c, half- and full-board or breakfast only (cheaper, but still **$$**, in hostel), thermal water in more expensive rooms, thermal pool, good restaurant, long-stay discounts, camping. Recommended. Also hydrothermal complex.

Camping
See **Termas de San Nicanor** and **Termas del Arapey** (both above), US$2.20 per person, good facilities.

Artigas *p49*
There are a few hotels in town.
$ Club Deportivo Artigas, Pte Berreta and LA de Herrera, 4 km from city, T4772 2532. Open all year, rooms and camping (see below), restaurant, no cooking facilities.

Camping

At **Club Zorrilla**, T4772 4341 and **Club Deportivo Artigas** (US$2.50 per person plus US$1.50 per tent).

---

❼ Restaurants

Colonia Suiza (Nueva Helvecia) p40

$$$-$$ Don Juan, main plaza. Snack bar/restaurant excellent food, pastries and bread.

Colonia del Sacramento p40, map p42

$$$ Buen Suspiro, Calle de los Suspiros 90, T4522 6160, www.buen suspiro.com. In the heart of the Old Town, wide selection of *picadas*, plenty of local wines, huge dessert menu. Very pleasant.

$$$ El Drugstore, Vasconcellos 179, T4522 5241. Hip, fusion food: Latin American, European, Japanese, good, creative varied menu, good salads and fresh vegetables. Music and show.

$$$ La Bodeguita, Del Comercio 167, T4522 5329. Daily 2030. Its terrace on the river is the main attraction of this lively pizza place that also serves good *chivitos* and pasta. Celebrating its 20th anniversary this year.

$$$ La Casa de Jorge Páez Vilaró, Misiones de los Tapes 65, T4522 9211. Closed Wed. Attractively set at an artist's former residence, it offers a short though varied and fine menu, only 8 tables.

$$$ La Florida, Odriozola 215, T094 293 036. Mediterranean and seafood dishes, outside seating.

$$$ Mesón de la Plaza, Vasconcellos 153, T4522 4807. 140-year-old house with a leafy courtyard, elegant dining, good traditional food.

$$$ Parrillada El Portón, Gral Flores 333, T4522 5318. Excellent *parrillada*. Small, relatively smart, good atmosphere. House speciality is offal and great sausages.

$$$ Pulpería de los Faroles, Misiones de los Tapes 101, T4523 0271. Inviting tables (candlelit at night) on the cobbled plaza, for a varied menu that includes tasty salads, seafood and local wines.

$$$ Punta Piedra, Ituzaingó y Gral Flores 248, T4522 2236. Daily 0900-0000. Set in a stone building, smart, great range of meat dishes, local wines, *parrilla*, *chivitos*, pastas.

$$$ Viejo Barrio (VB), Vasconcellos 169, T4522 5399. Closed Wed. Very good for home-made pastas and fish, renowned live shows.

$$$-$$ El Torreón, end of Av Gral Flores, T4523 1524. One of the best places to enjoy a sunset meal with views of the river. Set in an historic tower with in- and outdoor seating. Also serves toasties and cakes.

$$$-$$ Mercosur, Gral Flores y Ituzaingó, T4522 4200. Popular, varied dishes. Also café serving home-made cakes. All-you-can-eat buffet US$18. Cash only, but accepts 5 currencies including euros.

$$ Club Colonia, Gral Flores 382, T4522 2189. Good value, frequented by locals, good sturdy grub, traditional Uruguayan fare.

$$ Tasca del Sur, Las Flores s/n. . Open daily from 1200 until late in high season. For a change from *parrilla* and pasta, this tiny place does excellent tacos, quesadillas and fajitas. The chef takes his time about things, but it's worth the wait. Recommended.

Arcoiris, Av Gral Flores at Plaz a 25 de Agosto. Open till 0130. Very good ice cream. Recommended.

Mercedes *p44*

$$$ Casa Bordó, Paysandú 654, T4532 9817. French-owned and an unmissable stopover on the routes of Uruguay.

$$$-$$ Parador La Rambla, Rambla Costanera y 18 de Julio, T4532 7337. For good Spanish-influenced meals on the riverside.

Fray Bentos *p45*

Several cafés and pizzerias on 18 de Julio near Plaza Constitución.

$$$ Wolves, at Barrio Anglo, T4562 3604. Good home-made pastas next to the museum.

$$$-$$ Juventud Unida, 18 de Julio 1130, T4562 3365. The restaurant of a local football club is a popular place for varied meals.

Paysandú *p45, map p46*

$$$ Artemio, 18 de Julio 1248. Simple, reputation for serving the "best food in town".

$$$ Los Tres Pinos, Av España 1474, T4724 1211, www.lostrespinos.com.uy. Very good *parrillada*, as well as pastas and fish. There's a wine cellar and events are programmed.

Salto *p47*

$$$ La Caldera, Uruguay 221, T4732 4648. Closed Mon lunchtime. Good *parrillada* and local wines, also seafood.

$$$ La Casa de Lamas, Chiazzaro 20, T4732 9376. Fish and home-made pasta.

$$$ La Trattoria, at Club de Uruguay, Uruguay 754, T4733 6660. Breakfast and good-value meals, especially excellent pasta.

O Shopping

Colonia del Sacramento *p40, map p42*

There's a large artist community, Uruguayan and international, with good galleries across town. **El Almacén**, Real 150, sells creative gifts. **Paseo del Sol**, Del Comercio 158, is a small commercial centre selling local gifts. **Oveja Negra**, De la Playa 114, is recommended for woollen clothes. Leather shops on **C Santa Rita**, next to the Yacht Club. At **Arteco**, Rambla de las Américas y Av Mihanovich (Real de San Carlos), and **Gadec**, on C San Miguel (opposite Puerta de la Ciudadela), local artisans sell their produce.

O What to do

Colonia Suiza (Nueva Helvecia) *p40*

Finca La Rosada, Federico Fisher s/n, Nueva Helvecia, T4554 7026, www. larosada.com.uy. A soft-fruit farm, famous for its blueberries, pick-your-own in season, offers tours with lunch or tea, plus local sites.

Colonia del Sacramento *p40, map p42*
City tours
City tours available with **Destino Viajes**, Gral Flores 341, T4522 5343, destinoviajes@adinet.com.uy. **Asociación Guías de Turismo de Colonia**, T4522 2309, www.asociacionguiascolonia.blogspot.com, organizes walking tours (1 hr, in Spanish, US$6.50, other languages US$8.75, book in advance) in the Barrio Histórico, daily 1100 and 1500 from tourist office next to Old Gate.

A new hop-on, hop-off city tour bus, run by **Buquebus**, www.busturistico.com.uy, stops at 10 different stops in and around Colonia, US$25 valid all day, first bus 1100, last 1900.

Wine tours
Bodega Cerros de San Juan, Ruta 21, Km 213.5, T2481 7200, www.loscerrosdesanjuan.com.uy. Tours of the vineyards and winery, wine tastings and typical *asado* lunch. **Bodegas Cordano**, Ruta 21, Km 257, T4542 7316, www.almacendelacapilla.wix.com/almacendelacapilla. Tours, wine tastings and/or lunch.

Carmelo *p44*
Wine tours
See also **Finca Narbona**, page 51. **Bodega El Legado**, Ramal Ruta 97, Colonia Estrella, T099 111 493. Tours, tastings and/or typical *asado* lunch. Advance booking required. **Posada Campotinto**, Camino de los Peregrinos s/n, Colonia Estrella, T4542 7744, www.posadacampotinto.com. Wine tours, wine and cheese tastings,

Tannat tasting in the moonlight, accommodation, fine dining, other activities.

Paysandú *p45, map p46*
Bodega Leonardo Falcone, Av Wilson Ferreira Aldunate y Young, T4722 7718, www.bodegaleonardofalcone.com.uy. Winery tours at one of Uruguay's finest wine makers.

⊖ Transport

Colonia Suiza (Nueva Helvecia) *p40*
Bus
To **Montevideo**, frequent, with **COT**, 2-2½ hrs, US$8.15; **Turil**, goes via Valdense; to **Colonia del Sacramento**, frequent, 1 hr, US$4. Local services between Colonia Valdense and Nueva Helvecia connect with Montevideo/Colonia del Sacramento buses.

Colonia del Sacramento *p40, map p42*
Bus
All buses leave from terminal on Av Buenos Aires esq Manuel de Lobo, 7 blocks east of the Barrio Histórico, between the ferry port and the petrol station (free luggage lockers, tourist info desk, ATM, exchange, café and internet). To **Montevideo**, several services daily, 2¼-2¾ hrs, **COT**, T4522 3121, **Chadre**, T4522 4734, and **Turil**, T4522 5246, from US$11.30. **Turil** to **Colonia Valdense**, 1 hr, US$4. **Chadre** to **Conchillas**, US$2.50. To **Carmelo**, 1½ hrs, **Chadre** and **Berrutti**, T4522 5301, US$5. **Chadre** to **Mercedes**, 3½ hrs, US$12, **Fray Bentos**, 4 hrs,

US$14.50, **Paysandú**, 6 hrs, US$21.50, and **Salto**, 8 hrs, US$29.40. **Nossar**, T4522 2934, to **Durazno**, 3 hrs, US$15.

Car
There are plenty of filling stations between Colonia and the capital. If driving north to Paysandú and Salto, especially on Route 3, fill up with fuel and drinking water at every opportunity as stations are few and far between. From Colonia to **Punta del Este** by-passing Montevideo: take Ruta 11 at Ecilda Paullier, passing through San José de Mayo, Santa Lucía and Canelones, joining the Interbalnearia at Km 46.

Car and bike hire In bus terminal: **Avis** (main hall), T4522 9842, from US$150 per day, **Hertz** (50 m from entrance), T4522 9851, from US$90 per day. **Thrifty** by port, also at Gral Flores 172, T4522 2939, where there are **bicycles** (US$3 per hr), **scooters** (US$7 per hr) and **golf buggies** (US$15 per hr) for hire, recommended as traffic is slow and easy to navigate.

Ferry
Book in advance for all sailings in summer. Fares and schedules are given under Montevideo, Transport, page 36. To **Buenos Aires**: from 5 crossings daily, with **Buquebus** (T130), cars carried. **Colonia Express**, office at the port, T4522 9676, www.colonia express.com, makes 2-3 crossings a day between Colonia and **Buenos Aires** (50 mins) in fast boats (no vehicles carried) with bus connections to/from Montevideo,

Punta del Este and Uruguayan towns. **Seacat**, www.seacatcolonia.com, 3 fast ferries to Buenos Aires, 1 hr, office in Colonia T4522 2919. **Note**: if coming from Buenos Aires, passports must be stamped and Argentine departure tax paid even if only visiting Colonia for 1 day.

Taxi
A Méndez y Gral Flores, T4522 2920. Taxi in the centre US$3.50 flat fee.

Carmelo *p44*
Bus and boat
To **Montevideo**, US$15.50-18, **Intertur**, **Chadre** and **Sabelín**. To **Fray Bentos** (US$9), **Salto** (US$23.50), with **Chadre** from main plaza 0655, 1540. To **Colonia**, see above. To **Buenos Aires**: via Tigre, across the Paraná delta, an interesting bus/boat ride past innumerable islands: **Cacciola** 2 a day; T2908 2244, www.cacciolaviajes.com, see Montevideo, page 37.

Mercedes *p44*
Bus
To **Paysandú**, with **Sabelín**, in bus terminal, 1½-2 hrs, US$8-9; also **Chadre** on the Montevideo–Bella Unión route. To **Montevideo**, US$18, 3½ hrs, **CUT**, **Agencia Central** and **Sabelín**. To **Gualeguaychú**, 2 hrs, US$10, **ETA CUT**, **Ciudad de Gualeguay** (not Sun).

Fray Bentos *p45*
Bus
Terminal at 18 de Julio y Blanes. To/from **Montevideo**, **CUT**, 4-5 hrs, US$20, also **Chadre** and **Agencia**

Central. To **Mercedes**, **ETA**, US$2, 5 daily (not Sun).

Crossing to Argentina:
Fray Bentos *p45*
Bus
To **Buenos Aires**, 4 hrs, US$38.50, **CITA**. To **Gualeguaychú**, 1½ hrs, US$7, **ETA CUT** (not Sun).

Paysandú *p45, map p46*
Bus
It can be hard to get a seat on buses going north. Terminal at Zorrilla y Artigas, T4722 3225. To/from **Montevideo**, US$24 (**Núñez/Viajes Cynsa, Copay**, T4722 2094, 4 a day, US$22.50), 5-6 hrs, also **Chadre** and **Agencia Central**. To **Salto**, Agencia Central, **Alonso**, T4733 3969, 1½-2 hrs, 9 a day, US$8. To **Rivera**, US$21, **Copay**, Mon-Sat 0400. To **Fray Bentos**, 2 a day, 2 hrs direct, US$8. To **Colonia** by **Chadre**, 0750, 1750, 6 hrs, US$20.

Crossing to Argentina:
Paysandú *p47*
Bus
To **Colón**, Copay, Río Uruguay, 45 mins-1 hr, US$5.

Salto *p47*
Bus
Terminal 15 blocks east of centre at Batlle y Blandengues, café, shopping centre, casa de cambio. Take taxi to centre. To/from **Montevideo**, 5½-7½ hrs, US$35-43 (**Norteño, Núñez, Agencia Central** and **Chadre**). Chadre, Cotabu and **Hernández** to **Termas del Arapey**, 1½ hrs, daily, US$5. Also **Agentur**, 1 to 2 a day, US$6, via C

Treinta y Tres. To **Bella Unión**, 2 hrs, US$12, 2 a day. To **Colonia**, 0555, 1555, 8 hrs, US$28; to **Fray Bentos**, same times, US$17.

Car hire
Maxicar, Paraguay 764, T4733 5554, 9943 5454, www.maxicarsalto.com. 24 hrs, cars allowed to travel to Argentina and Brazil.

Crossing to Argentina *p47*
Bus
To **Concordia**, **Chadre** and **Flecha Bus**, 2 a day each Mon-Fri, 2 on Sat, no buses Sun, US$5, 1¼-1½ hrs. To **Buenos Aires**, US$45, **Flecha Bus**.

Launch
To **Concordia**, US$4, 15 mins, 4 a day (not Sun), depart port on C Brasil; immigration either side of river, quick and easy.

Artigas *p49*
Bus
To **Salto**, COA, T4772 2268, US$15. **Turil** and **COT** from **Montevideo** 7-7½ hrs, US$42 via Durazno, Paso de los Toros and Tacuarembó.

● Directory

Colonia del Sacramento *p40, map p42*
Banks Banks open afternoon only. Most museums and restaurants accept Argentine pesos or US dollars, but rarely euros. **HSBC**, De Portugal 183 (Barrio Histórico), Mon-Fri 1300-1700. **Cambio Dromer**, Gral Flores 350, T4522 2070, Mon-Fri 1000-1800,

Sat 1000-1700 (branch at **Casino Radisson** daily 1400-0400). **Cambio Colonia** and **Western Union**, Gral Flores y Lavalleja, T4522 5032.
Consulates Argentine Consulate and Cultural Centre, Gral Flores 209, T4522 2093, open weekdays 1300-1800.

Paysandú *p45, map p46*
Banks Casas de cambio on 18 de Julio: **Cambio Fagalde**, No 1004;

Cambio Bacacay, No 1039; change TCs, Sat 0830-1230.
Consulates Argentina, Gómez 1034, T4722 2253, Mon-Fri 1300-1800.

Salto *p47*
Banks Casas de cambio on C Uruguay. **Consulates** Argentina, Artigas 1162, T4733 2931, Mon-Fri 0900-1400.

Eastern Uruguay

Resorts line the coast from Montevideo to Punta del Este, the ultimate magnet for summer holidaymakers, especially from Argentina. Out of season, it is quieter and you can have the beaches to yourself, which is pretty much the case the closer you get to Brazil year round. Inland are cattle ranches, some of which welcome visitors, as well as quiet lagoons and hills with expansive views.

The beautiful coast east of Montevideo consists of an endless succession of small bays, beaches and promontories, set among hills and woodlands. The beach season runs from December to the end of February. An excellent four-lane highway leads to Punta del Este and Rocha, and a good two-lane highway to Chuy, near the Brazilian border. This route takes in the most important Uruguayan beach resorts, as well as Parque Nacional Santa Teresa and other natural attractions. If driving, there are four tolls each way (about US$2.40 each), but this route is the easiest and the most comfortable in Uruguay with sufficient service stations along the way.

Piriápolis → *For listings, see pages 73-84. Population: 8830.*

This resort set among hills, 101 km from Montevideo, is laid out with an abundance of shady trees, and the district is rich in pine, eucalyptus and acacia woods. It has a good beach, a yacht harbour, a country club, a motor-racing track (street circuit) and is particularly popular with Argentines. It was, in fact, founded in the 1890s as a bathing resort for residents of Buenos Aires. Next to the marina is a small cable car (with seats for two) to the top of **Cerro San Antonio** ① *US$4, 10 mins' ride, free car park and toilets at lower station,* for magnificent views of Piriápolis and its beaches. Recommended, but be careful when disembarking. It can also be reached by car, bus or on foot, and there are several restaurants at the top. North of the town centre, at **Punta de Playa Colorada**, is a marine rescue centre ① *www.sosfaunamarina.com,* that looks after injured sea creatures before releasing them to the wild. For **tourist information**, head to the Asociación de Turismo ① *Paseo de la Pasiva, Rambla de los Argentinos, summer 0900-2400, winter 1000-1800, T4432 5055, www.destinopiriapolis.com.*

Just north of Piriápolis R 37 passes the **La Cascada** municipal park (open all year, small waterfall, old woodlands, picnic area, toilets) which contains the grand 19th-century house of Francisco Piria, the founder of the resort, and the **Museo Castillo de Piria** ① *open daily in summer, 1000-1730 (winter Tue-Sun 1000-1530), free.*

About 6 km north of Piriápolis on the R37 is **Cerro Pan de Azúcar** (Sugar Loaf Hill), crowned by a tall cross with a circular stairway inside; fine coastal views. There is only a steep path, marked by red arrows, up to the cross. To get there, take the bus 'Cerro Pan de Azúcar' and get off after 6 km. About 4 km beyond Cerro Pan de Azúcar is the village of Pan de Azúcar, which has a **Museo al Aire Libre de Pintura** where the walls of the buildings have been decorated by Uruguayan and Argentine painters, designers and writers with humorous and tango themes; this is known as the **Mural Circuit** (direct bus every hour from Piriápolis).

Portezuelo and Punta Ballena → *For listings, see pages 73-84.*

R93 runs between the coast and the Laguna del Sauce to Portezuelo, which has good beaches. The **Arboreto Lussich** ① *T4257 8077, 1000-1800, free,* on the west slope of the Sierra de la Ballena (north of R93) contains a unique set of native and exotic trees. There are footpaths, or you can drive through and two miradors; it's worth a visit. From Portezuelo drive north towards the R9 by way of the R12 which then continues, unpaved, to Minas. Just off the R12 is **El Tambo Lapataia** ① *1 km east from Solanas, then 4 km north, T4222 0303,* *www.lapataiapuntadeleste.com,* a dairy farm open to the public, selling cheese, ice cream, *dulce de leche,* home-made pizzas and pastas. There are also farming activities and an organic garden.

At Punta Ballena there is a wide crescent beach, calm water and very clean sand. The place is a residential resort but is still quiet. At the top of Punta Ballena there is a panoramic road 2.5 km long with remarkable views of the coast. **Casa Pueblo** ⓘ *www.carlospaezvilaro.com.uy, gallery open all year daily, 1000-sunset, US$6,* the house and gallery of Uruguayan artist Carlos Páez Vilaró who passed away in 2014, is built in a Spanish-Moroccan style on a cliff over the sea; the gallery can be visited, there are paintings, collages and ceramics on display, and for sale. Walk downhill towards the sea for a good view of the house.

Maldonado → *For listings, see pages 73-84. Population: 65,865.*

The capital of Maldonado Department, 140 km east of Montevideo, is a peaceful town, sacked by the British in 1806. It has many colonial remains and the historic centre has been restored. It is also a dormitory suburb of Punta del Este. Worth seeing is the **El Vigía watch tower** ⓘ *Michelini y Pérez del Puerto;* the **Cathedral** ⓘ *Plaza San Fernando,* which was started in 1801 and completed in 1895; the **windmill**; the **Cuartel de Dragones exhibition centre** ⓘ *Pérez del Puerto y 18 de Julio, by Plaza San Fernando,* and the **Cachimba del Rey** ⓘ *on the continuation of 3 de Febrero, almost Artigas,* an old well – legend claims that those who drink from it will never leave Maldonado. **Museo Mazzoni** ⓘ *Ituzaingó 789, T4222 1107, summer 0800-2200, winter 1300-1800, free,* has regional items, indigenous, Spanish, Portuguese and English. **Museo de Arte Americano** ⓘ *Treinta y Tres 823 y Dodera, T4222 2276, http://maam-uruguay.blogspot.com, 1800-2200, Dec and Feb Fri-Sun only (closed winter),* is an interesting private museum of national and international art. For tourist information, do to the **Dirección General de Turismo** ⓘ *Edif Municipal, T4222 3333, www.maldonado.gub.uy.*

Punta del Este → *For listings, see pages 73-84. Population: 9200.*

About 7 km from Maldonado and 139 km from Montevideo (a little less by dual carriageway), facing the bay on one side and the open waters of the Atlantic on the other, lies the largest and best known of the resorts, Punta del Este, part of the municipality of Maldonado and particularly popular among Argentines and Brazilians. The narrow peninsula of Punta del Este has been entirely built over and is now more of a service centre for visitors, with fewer people choosing to stay on the peninsula itself. On the land side, the city is flanked by large planted forests of eucalyptus, pine and mimosa. Two blocks from the sea, at the tip of the peninsula, is the historic monument of **El Faro** (lighthouse); in this part of the city no building may exceed its height. On the ocean side of the peninsula, at the end of Calle 25 (Arrecifes), is a shrine to the first Mass said by the conquistadors on this coast, 2 February 1515. Three blocks from the shrine is Plaza General Artigas, which has a *feria artesanal* (handicraft market); along its side runs Avenida Gorlero, the main street. There are two casinos, a golf course, and many beautiful holiday houses. **Museo Ralli of Contemporary Latin American Art** ⓘ *Curupay y Los Arrayanes s/n, Barrio Beverly Hills, T4248 3476, www.museoralli.com.uy, Tue-Sun 1400-1800 closed Jun-Sep, free,* is worth a visit but a car (or bike – cycle path all the way from Punta del Este) is needed.

Tourist information ⓘ *Liga de Fomento, Parada 1, T4244 6519, open summer 0800-1800, winter 1100-1700; in bus station T4249 4042; at Rambla Claudio Williman (Mansa side), T4223 0050; at Plaza Artigas, Av Gorlero, T4244 6510; and at airports.* See also the websites www.puntaweb.com, www.puntadeleste.com and www.vivapunta.com.

Beaches and islands

Punta del Este has excellent bathing beaches, the calm Playa Mansa on the bay side, the rough Playa Brava on the ocean side. There are some small beaches hemmed in by rocks on this side of the peninsula, but most

Punta del Este

Where to stay
Agupy 1
Conrad Hotel y Casino 2
El Viajero Brava
Beach Hostel 3
El Viajero Manantiales
Hostel 4
Gaudí 5
Iberia 6
Punta del Este Hostel 7
Remanso 8
Tánger 9

Restaurants
Gure-etxe 3
Il Barreto 4
Isidora 5
La Bourgogne 1
Lo de Charlie 7
Lo de Tere 8
Los Caracoles 9
Viejo Marino 10
Yatch Club Uruguayo 12

Luxury tourism

Uruguay might seem an unlikely place for luxury tourism to take off, but that's exactly what's happened in recent years. The current president, José Mujica, has made it easier for foreigners to settle here and get Uruguayan residency, something that's encouraged investment from foreign entrepreneurs, who are behind several of the luxury tourism ventures. Punta del Este and surrounding beaches have long had a reputation as a luxury destination, but now luxury tourism is spreading and branching out to include smaller resorts along the Atlantic coastline, particularly José Ignacio, a few kilometres to the north, but also Montevideo, Colonia del Sacramento, Carmelo and further inland. Luxury accommodation has perhaps received the most investment, with a number of new, or restored, properties opening, including the magnificent casino at Carrasco, in Montevideo, a 100-year-old building restored to its former glory over a three-year period (www. sofitel.com). Also in Montevideo,

Esplendor Boutique Hotel (www.esplendormontevideo.com), in the former Hotel Cervantes, offers avant-garde design on the outskirts of the Old Town. Although things are happening in the capital, Uruguay's endless beaches, following the coastline all the way up to Brazil, have seen the most luxury developments, many of which are in or near José Ignacio, a former fishing village with a laid-back vibe and plenty of modern art. It's home to three luxury Vik properties, two on the beach, one – an estancia – inland (www.vikretreats.com). Also in and around José Ignacio are a further three luxury properties: **Fasano Las Piedras** (www.laspiedrasfasano. com), **Casa Suaya** (www.casasuaya. com) and **Posada Azul Marino** (www.azulmarino.com.uy).

Fine dining is following suit, with an increasing number of elegant restaurant options, making the most of local produce and traditional Uruguayan fare with an innovative twist. The wine regions also have several options, including staying at a wine *finca* (see box, page 35).

people go to where the extensive Playa Brava starts. **Papa Charlie** beach on the Atlantic (Parada 13) is preferred by families with small children as it is safe. Quieter beaches are at **La Barra** and beyond.

There is an excellent yacht marina, yacht and fishing clubs. There is good fishing both at sea and in three nearby lakes and the Río Maldonado.

Isla de Gorriti ⓘ *0800-1830, 0900-1700 in winter, entry US$13.50; boats from 0930-1700, return 1015-1815, US$15, T4244 6166; Don Quico Cruceros, also does fishing trips, T4244 8945),* visited by explorers including Solís, Magellan and Drake, was heavily fortified by the Spanish in the 1760s to keep the Portuguese out. It is densely wooded, with superb beaches and is an ideal spot for campers. On **Isla de Lobos**, which is a government reserve within sight of the town, there is a huge sea-lion colony; public boat US$20 per person (leaves 1200), tour US$30-50. Tickets should be booked in advance (T4244 1716, or **Dimartours** T4244 4750, www.dimartours.com.uy).

Maldonado eastern beaches → *For listings, see pages 73-84.*

Between the peninsula and the mouth of the Río Maldonado, a road runs along the coast, passing luxurious houses, dunes and pines. Some of the most renowned architects of Uruguay and Argentina design houses here. Several of the beaches east of Punta del Este are excellent for surfing, more so the further east towards Brazil you travel.

La Barra and around

First in line after the main resort is La Barra, a fashionable, very hip and happening place, especially for summer nightlife. With Punta del Este 'downtown' (on the peninsula), increasingly turning into a service centre, many visitors are choosing to base themselves here or in other, less built-up beach resorts. La Barra has a good collection of beaches, art galleries, bars and restaurants (take a bus from Punta del Este terminal or taxi US$20). The **Museo del Mar Sirenamis** ① *1 km off the coast road, watch for signs, T4277 1817, www. museodelmar.com.uy, summer daily 1030-2030 winter 1100-1700, US$7*, has an extensive collection on the subject of the sea, its life and history and on the first beach resorts. The coast road climbs a headland here before descending to the beaches further north, Montoya and **Manantiales** (reached by Condesa bus; taxi US$30). Further inland lies **Fundación Pablo Atchugarry** ① *Ruta 104, Km 4.5, El Chorro, T4277 5563, www.fundacionpabloatchugarry.org, daily Dec-Mar 1000-2200, Apr-Nov 1100-1900, free*, a multi-function art gallery and sculpture park, close to nature. Events are regularly organized.

José Ignacio

Some 30 km along the coast from Punta del Este is the former fishing village of José Ignacio. In recent years it has become home to an increasingly glamorous, alternative and arty crowd. The old **lighthouse** ① *summer daily 1100-2030, winter 1100-1330, 1430-1830, US$0.75*, still attracts many visitors, but this is no longer the humble fishing village it was 10 years ago. These days there are plenty of new developments of the five-star kind, but against the odds this small beach resort retains a laid-back fishing village vibe, perhaps because the new luxury developments are exceedingly laid-back too. There are several new noteworthy restaurants and bars, with excellent locations right on the beach, small shops and cafés, a beach club and, for such a small place (about 300 permanent residents), an abundance of art. Expect to find galleries, organic food, yoga classes and estate agents. Coastal R10 is now all paved and continues east of José Ignacio to La Paloma and north towards the Brazilian border.

Pueblo Garzón

Inland from José Ignacio, near Laguna Garzón and off Ruta 9, lies Pueblo Garzón, a small village of less than 300 inhabitants that's experiencing something of a boom in culinary tourism. It's home to one of the finest restaurants in Uruguay (see page 80), but this is also the place to sample local wines and olive oil, or simply stroll the quiet streets of the village, that are nicely preserved. Nearby **Laguna Garzón** is good for birdwatching.

Department of Rocha beaches → *For listings, see pages 73-84.*

La Paloma and around → *Population: 3554.*

Protected by an island and a sandspit, this is a good port for yachts. The surrounding scenery is attractive, with extensive wetlands nearby. You can walk for miles along the beach. The **tourist office** ① *in La Paloma bus station, T9995 6662*, is very helpful. There's also a **Department of Rocha office** ① *Rutas 9 y 15, daily 0800-2000, T4472 3100, www.turismorocha.gub.uy*. Nearby **Laguna de Rocha** is excellent for birdwatching, canoeing and bike rides (tours organized by **Lares**, see Montevideo, What to do, page 34).

Coastal R10 continues to La Pedrera, Cabo Polonio, Aguas Dulces and other places of interest along the coast (regular bus services, **Rutas del Sol**, cover the whole coast along Rutas 9, 10 and 16).

La Pedrera

About 10 km from La Paloma is La Pedrera, a beautiful village overlooking two bays with stunning views and sandy beaches. Just like most of the smaller (former) fishing villages along the coast east of Punta del Este, La Pedrera is attracting more visitors, and is consequently slowly increasing in size. The majority of these smaller resorts is so far mostly attracting national/local visitors, some Argentineans and Brazilians, but fewer other international visitors – a sprinkling of Spanish comes in handy here. The centre of La Pedrera sits high on a cliff overlooking two long, sandy bays, excellent for surfing. Most amenities are centred along Avenida Principal, running from the roundabout where buses drop passengers off, right down to the seafront (a five- to10-minute walk). Although slowly becoming more built up, La Pedrera is surrounded by lush vegetation inland and several hotels and guesthouses have chosen to keep these surroundings as intact as possible, allowing people to stay in a forested environment. A number of pleasant bars and restaurants can be found along the Rambla, overlooking the sea.

Barra de Valizas and around

Beyond La Pedrera the road runs towards Barra de Valizas, a small, very laid-back hide-away. This little gem of a beach resort is similar to Punta del Diablo further north (see page 68), with a gently hippified vibe. The permanent population is no more than 300 souls, but in high season, December to March, it swells and comes alive. It's also far more economical than most places along the coast – so far there are no hotels, only hostels, camping and a few posadas, which are the most upmarket and comfortable option. Calle Principal runs one block from the small bus station down towards the sea, and is home to most of the facilities, including a friendly cybercafé, one of few places to be open year-round. There is also a **Plaza de Artesanos** on Calle Principal with interesting handicrafts, including ceramics. Above all, Valizas has a friendly vibe, popular with young people, but by no means exclusively so. The enticing beaches have lifeguards in high season. It's possible to walk all the way from Valizas to Cabo Polonio across spectacular sand dunes (three to four hours, take sun screen and plenty of water). To reach the sand dunes, take a short boat ride across the stream that separates them from the main beach at the southern end of the village (US$1.30 return, several fishermen wait at the end of the beach to take you across and back). A walk across the dunes gives excellent views over the sea and nearby lagoons (swimming possible in both sea and lagoons).

Cabo Polonio (permanent population 80) has two great beaches: the north beach is more rugged, while the south is tamer by comparison. Both have lifeguards on duty (though their zone of protection only covers a tiny portion of the endless stretches of beach). The whole cape is part of a national park, which limits the number of people who are allowed to stay; the number of lodgings is limited and camping is strictly forbidden (if you arrive with a tent, it may be confiscated). During January or February (and especially during Carnival), you have to reserve a room in one of the few posadas or hotels, or better yet, rent a house (see Where to stay, page 76). From Km 264 on the main road all-terrain vehicles run 8 km across the dunes to the village (several companies, around US$5; the tourist office by the terminal is open 1000-1800, T9996 8747). Day visitors must leave just after sundown (see Transport, page 83).

The **Monte de Ombúes** ⓘ *open in summer months, from Jan, free, basic restaurant with honest prices,* is a wood containing a few *ombú* trees (*Phytolacca dioica* – the national tree), *coronilla* (*Scutia buxifolia*) and *canelón* (*Rapanea laetevirens*). It has a small circuit to follow and a good hide for birdwatching. To reach the woods from Km 264, go 2 km north along the R10 to the bridge. Here take a boat with guide, 30 minutes along the river (**Monte Grande,** montegrande@adinet.com.uy, are recommended as they visit both sides of the river). You can also walk from Km 264 across the fields, but it's a long way and the last 150 m are through thick brush. The bridge is 16 km from Castillos on the R9 (see next paragraph): turn onto the R16 towards Aguas Dulces, just before which you turn southwest onto the R10.

From **Aguas Dulces** the road runs inland to the pleasant town of **Castillos**. A small centre for the region, it has ATM, shops, taxi rank and bus terminal, all on the leafy main square. There are colourfully painted houses, some with murals. From here you can get bus connections to Chuy. A **tourist office** ① *T9981 7068, open 1000-1300, 1700-2200*, at the Aguas Dulces/Castillos crossroads on the R9, has details on hotels.

Punta del Diablo

At Km 298 there is a turn-off to an increasingly touristy fishing village in dramatic surroundings of impressive sand dunes. Punta del Diablo is quite spread out, both inland and along its three fine beaches, **Playa de la Viuda** to the south, **Playa del Pescador** in the centre and **Playa del Rivero** to the north (running into **Playa Grande**, which partly lies inside Santa Teresa national park). The bus station, which also has tourist information, is about 2 km out of town. The centre, on the other hand, is compact and concentrated around a few streets near Playa del Pescador. Punta del Diablo is very rustic and ramshackle with a gentle hippie vibe. Brightly painted, colourful houses add to its charm. It's great for surfing and popular with young people in high season, but from April to November the solitude and the dramatically lower prices make it a wonderful getaway for couples or families. The streets near Playa del Pescador and the main street, San Martín, have a number of amenities from supermarkets and bars to cafés and a bookshop. There are also plenty of seasonal stalls and sheds, selling everything from freshly baked *empanadas* to henna tattoos. Increased popularity has brought more lodging (you can choose between hostels, hotels, *cabañas* and self-catering flats or even large-scale family houses) and services year-round, although off-season is still extremely quiet compared to summer. Despite the holidaymakers, Punta del Diablo is still a working fishing village and every morning the small boats head out from, and then return to, Playa del Pescador with freshly caught fish and seafood. The day's catch can be bought from small shacks near the fishing boats if you have your own kitchen, or enjoyed in some of the nearby eateries. There's a **Municipal tourist office** ① *T4477 2412, daily 0800-2200*, and you can consult www.portaldeldiablo.com. There is now an ATM, as well as other amenities, in the northern part of town near Playa del Rivero.

Parque Nacional Santa Teresa → *For listings, see pages 73-84.*

Arriving in the park
The park is 100 km from Rocha, 308 km from Montevideo, and is open 0800-2000 to day visitors (open 24 hours for campers), T4477 2101/03 ext 209. Entrance is free.

Visiting the park
This park has curving, palm-lined avenues and plantations of many exotic trees. It also contains botanical gardens, freshwater pools for bathing and beaches which stretch for many kilometres (the surf is too rough for swimming). It is the site of the impressive colonial fortress of Santa Teresa, begun by the Portuguese in 1762 and seized by the Spanish in 1793. The fortress houses a **museum** ① *Wed-Sun 1300-1900 (winter Fri-Sun 1200-1800), US$1*, with artefacts from the wars of Independence. There's an old cemetery nearby, as well as several cafés and snack bars that open during the high season. On the inland side of Route 9, the strange and gloomy Laguna Negra and the marshes of the Bañado de Santa Teresa support large numbers of wild birds (tours are organized by **Lares**, see Montevideo, page 34). A road encircles the fortress; it's possible to drive or walk around even after closing. From the fortress there is a good view of Laguna Negra.

There are countless campsites (open all year), and a few cottages to let in the summer (usually snapped up quickly). At the Capatacía, or administrative headquarters, campers pay US$4 per person per night. The park is well kept, with good facilities and plenty of space. Facilities are usually attached to the different campsites and include cafés, supermarkets, telephones, post office, laundry services and several small restaurants. Most sites have excellent *parrilla* facilities for private use, but take extra care if using these. Fires have been a hazard in the past, with a large-scale fire devastating parts of the park in 2005, and it now has its own small fire brigade. Beautiful isolated beaches abound all along the park's coastline. At **Playa de la Moza**, one of the main beaches, there's also a small hostel recently opened and **El Chorro**, a natural pool, nice for a refreshing swim. There are several recommended walks throughout the park; both **Camino del Soldado** and **Barrancas Coloradas** are pleasant walks through deeply forested areas, 1.5-2 km each. Ask at the Capatacía for routes. Near the Capatacía there is a small botanical garden, as well as a large children's playground with mini-zoo and aviary. Practically every amenity is closed off-season. The bathing resort of **La Coronilla** is 10 km north of Santa Teresa, 20 km south of Chuy; it has the **Karumbé** ① *Ruta 9, Km 314, T09-991 7811, www.karumbe.org, Jan-Apr 1000-1900*, a marine turtle centre. There are several hotels and restaurants, most closed in winter (tourist information T9977 7129). Montevideo–Chuy buses stop at La Coronilla.

Parque Nacional Santa Teresa

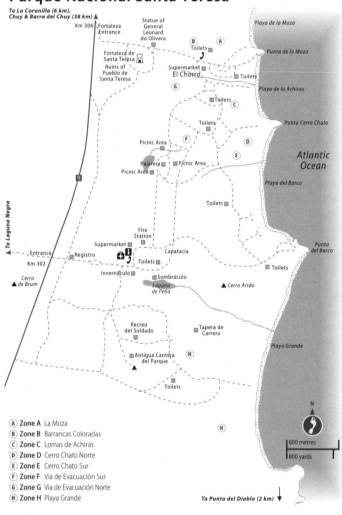

To La Coronilla (6 km),
Chuy & Barra del Chuy (38 km)

Km 306 Fortaleza Entrance

Statue of General Leonard do Olivera

Playa de la Moza

Punta de la Moza

Ⓑ Ⓐ Toilets

Fortaleza de Santa Teresa

Ruins of Pueblo de Santa Teresa

Supermarket
El Chorro

Toilets

Playa de la Achiras

Ⓖ

Toilets

Ⓒ

Punta Cerro Chato

Toilets

Ⓕ

Picnic Area

Ⓓ

Atlantic Ocean

Pajarera

Picnic Area

Ⓔ

Picnic Area

Playa del Barco

Toilets

Fire Station

Punta del Barco

Supermarket

Capatacía

To Laguna Negra

Entrance
Km 302

Registro

Toilets

Toilets

Cerro de Brum

Invernáculo

Sombráculo

Laguna de Peña

▲ Cerro Arido

Recreo del Soldado

Tapera de Carrero

Playa Grande

Ⓗ

Antigua Cantera del Parque

Toilets

N

800 metres
800 yards

Ⓐ **Zone A** La Moza
Ⓑ **Zone B** Barrancas Coloradas
Ⓒ **Zone C** Lomas de Achiras
Ⓓ **Zone D** Cerro Chato Norte
Ⓔ **Zone E** Cerro Chato Sur
Ⓕ **Zone F** Via de Evacuación Sur
Ⓖ **Zone G** Via de Evacuación Norte
Ⓗ **Zone H** Playa Grande

To Punta del Diablo (2 km)

Wreckers, revolutionaries and gauchos

Uruguay's passion for rural life began in 1603 with Hernando Arias and the first shipment of cattle and horses to the Banda Oriental.

Today, a typical day on an estancia begins at the hearth, perhaps with a warming *mate*, before a horse ride. The fireplace may be decorated with signs of present and past ownership, each brand burnt into the fireplace representing a personal history, but one element unites them all: the myth of the gaucho.

You might be forgiven for imagining yourself a latter-day gaucho as you put your foot in the *copa* (a cupped stirrup) and mount a sturdy Uruguayan horse, perhaps of the same breed as the one that Napoleon had shipped back to carry him around a wintry Europe. However, your thick poncho might well be the only piece of gaucho gear that you are wearing. Gauchos sometimes used ponchos as shields in knife fights, but on the ride you probably won't be needing a *facón* (a large dagger), nor a pair of *bombachas* (baggy trousers gathered at the ankle) or *culero* (an apron of soft leather tied around the waist, open on the left side) to avoid lacerations from a lasso during branding and gelding. Horses on tourism estancias are used to novice riders, and *rebenques* (short whips) are best kept unused by your side. You'll find the Uruguayan horse a compliant platform for launching your *boleadoras* (three stones, covered with hide, on ropes tied at the middle, which are used for entangling the legs of cattle). At this point you may learn whether your horse is a *pingo*, a gaucho's favourite horse, or *flete*, an ordinary cargo beast.

Riding along extensive *cuchillas* (ridges) and crossing rivers will bring to mind the nomadic gaucho lifestyle, and the revolutionary (largely gaucho) guerrilla bands. A *montonera* was a band of gauchos organized to drive the Brazilians and Argentinians out of Uruguay. Patriot leader Artigas was a gaucho-*caudillo* (boss).

Uruguayan life is built from livestock, sometimes quite literally. Houses were occasionally made from cattle hide. And cattle were put to other uses: coastal ranchers in Maldonado Department in the 19th century placed lights on the horns of their cows to lure ships onto the rocks for plunder.

Chuy → *For listings, see pages 73-84. Population: 11,037.*

At Chuy, 340 km from Montevideo, the Brazilian frontier runs along the main street, Avenida Internacional, which is called Avenida Brasil in Uruguay and Avenida Uruguaí in Brasil. The Uruguayan side has more services, including supermarkets, duty-free shops and a casino. The **tourist office** ① *T4474*

3627, infochuy@turismorocha.gub.uy, 0900-2200, is on the plaza. See also www.chuynet.com.

On the Uruguayan side, on a promontory overlooking Laguna Merín and the gaucho landscape of southern Brazil, stands the restored fortress of **San Miguel** ① *Wed-Sun 1300-1900 (high season), Thu-Sun 1300-1900 (low season), US$0.90*, dating from 1734, with four bastions and surrounded by a moat. Back in 1930 the fortress was in ruins, but largely thanks to the efforts of one man, historian Horacio Arredondo, a large-scale restoration project was undertaken and today the fortress is well worth a visit. Each room within the building has been carefully restored and you can visit everything from the small chapel to the officers' mess. The fortress is set above a 1500-ha wetland park, which is good for birdwatching and is 10 km north of Chuy along Route 19 which is the border. There is a small museum of *criollo* and *indígena* culture (entrance included in the fortress ticket), displaying, among other artefacts, old carriages and presses, as well as a permanent exhibition dedicated to Horacio Arredondo and the restoration of the fortress. The museum is not always open in low season. A fine walk from here is 2 km to the Cerro Picudo. The path starts behind the museum, very apparent. Tours (US$10 from Chuy) end for the season after 31 March. A bus from Chuy costs US$1.50, **Rutas del Sol** buses from Montevideo go here after passing through Chuy.

Border with Brazil

Uruguayan passport control is 2.5 km before the border on Ruta 9 into Chuy, US$2 by taxi, 20 minutes' walk, or take a town bus; the officials are friendly and cooperative. Ministry of Tourism kiosk here (T4474 4599) is helpful, especially for motorists. Tourists may freely cross the border in either direction as long as they do not go beyond either country's border post. Taking a car into Brazil is no problem if the car is not registered in Brazil or Uruguay. Uruguayan rental cars are not allowed out of the country; although you can freely drive between Chuy and Chuí, if you break down/have an accident on the Brazilian side, car rental insurance will not cover it; park in Chuy, even if only 1 m from Brazil, and then walk.) From the border post, Ruta 9 bypasses the town, becoming BR-471 on the Brazilian side, leading to Brazilian immigration, also outside town. The Brazilian consulate is at Tito Fernández 147, T4474 2049, Chuy, open 0900-1300. For buses to Brazilian destinations, go to the *rodoviária* in Chuí. The bus companies that run from Chuy into Brazil ask for passports – make sure you get yours back before boarding the bus.

Entering Uruguay You need a Brazilian exit stamp and a Uruguayan entry stamp (unless visiting only Chuí), otherwise you'll be turned back at customs or other official posts. Those requiring a visa will be charged around US$80 depending on the country.

◉Eastern Uruguay listings

For hotel and restaurant price codes and other relevant information, see pages 10-12.

◉ Where to stay

Piriápolis *p61*
Most hotels along the seafront close end Feb to mid-Dec. Book in advance in high season. There are many more than those listed here.

$$$ pp Argentino Hotel, Rambla de los Argentinos y Armenia, T4432 2791, www.argentinohotel.com.uy. A fine hotel and landmark designed by Piria with casino, 2 restaurants, medicinal springs, sauna and good facilities for children and teenagers.

$$$ Escorial, Rambla de los Argentinos 1290, T4432 2537, www.hotelescorial.com. With mini-bar, safe in room, pool, parking, children's playground, laundry service.

$$$-$$ Rivadavia, Rambla de los Argentinos y Trápani, T4432 2532, www.hotelrivadavia.com. Open all year (much cheaper in winter). Restaurant, parking.

$ pp Hostel Piriápolis, Simón del Pino 1136 y Tucumán, T4432 0394, www.hostelpiriapolis.com.uy. Rooms for 2-4 (open all year), private rooms **$$**, 240 beds, non-HI members pay more, hot showers, cooking facilities, student cards accepted.

Camping
El Toro, Av de Mayo y Fuente de Venus, T4432 3454. Doubles in bungalows, and tents.

Piriápolis Fútbol Club, Misiones y Niza, just behind bus station, T4432 3275, piriapolisfc@adinet.com.uy. US$5.75.

Portezuelo and Punta Ballena *p61*
$$$$ Casa Pueblo, T4257 8611, www.clubhotelcasapueblo.com. Highly recommended hotel and apartments, spa and, lower down the hill, restaurant **Las Terrazas**.

$$$$ Hotel-Art Las Cumbres, Ruta 12, Km 3.5, 4 km inland, T4257 8689, www.cumbres.com.uy. Themed as an artist's house-studio, on a wooded hill with great views over Laguna del Sauce and the coast, highly regarded, pool, restaurant and tea room (expensive but popular).

$$$$ Serena Hotel, Rambla Williman parada 24, T4223 3441, www.serena hoteles.com. Design hotel, adults only, in- and outdoor swimming pools, spa and several restaurants, on Playa Mansa.

Campsite
Punta Ballena, Km 120, Parada 45, T4257 8902, www.campingpunta ballena.com. US$11.50 per person per night (US$9 in low season), many facilities, very clean. Also has tents for hire, US$4.50 tent only, and cabins for 4-8 people (**$$$**).

Maldonado *p62*
Hotel accommodation is scarce in summer; cheaper than Punta del Este, but you will have to commute to the beach.

\$\$\$-\$\$ Colonial, 18 de Julio 841 y Florida, T4222 3346, www.colonialhotel.com.uy.
\$\$ Catedral, Florida 830 casi 18 de Julio, T4224 2513, www.hotel catedral.com.uy. Central.
\$\$ Celta, Ituzaingó 839, T4223 0139. Helpful, Irish owner, No 7 bus stop outside.
\$\$ Isla de Gorriti, Michelini 884, T4224 5218. Nice courtyard. Recommended.

Camping
El Edén, Balneario Las Flores, T4438 0565, www.eledencamping.com. US\$9, also has *cabañas* for 2-6 people.

Punta del Este *p62, map p63*
Note Streets on the peninsula have names and numbers; lowest numbers at the tip. Hotels are plentiful but expensive; we list recommended ones only. Rates in the few hotels still open after the end of Mar are often halved. To avoid spending a fortune on taxis, visitors without a car should stay at a hotel on the peninsula.

On the peninsula
\$\$\$\$ Conrad Hotel y Casino, Parada 4, Playa Mansa, T4249 1111, www.conrad.com.uy. Luxurious hotel with spa, concerts and events, wonderful views. Book in advance in high season.
\$\$\$\$ Iberia, Calle 24, No 685, T4244 0405, www.iberiahotel.com.uy. With disabled access and garage opposite. **\$\$\$** in the low season.
\$\$\$\$ Remanso, Calle 20 y 28, T4244 7412, www.hotelremanso.com.uy. Comfortable, businesslike, pool, jacuzzi, safe, open all year. 2- to 4-bed rooms (also 2 more expensive suites). Some rooms **\$\$\$** in the low season. Recommended.
\$\$\$\$-\$\$\$ Tánger, Calle 31 entre 18 y 20, T4244 1333, www.hoteltanger.com. Closed May-Aug. More expensive in highest season, safe, disabled access, 2 pools.
\$\$\$-\$\$ El Viajero Brava Beach Hostel and Suites, Av Francia y Charrúa, T4248 0331, www.elviajero bravabeach.com. Private en suite with TV, dorms (**\$**) with a/c, breakfast included, cable TV and DVDs, bar, fireplace, free Wi-Fi.
\$\$\$-\$\$ Gaudí, C Risso, parada 1, by bus terminal, T4249 4116, www.hotelgaudi.com.uy. Open all year. 2-star. Good, convenient, safe, fridge, bar.
\$\$-\$ Agupy (formerly **1949 Hostel**), Esq 30 y 18, T4244 0719. Close to the bus terminal and beaches. New ownership. Rooms with sea view.
\$ pp Punta del Este Hostel, C 25 No 544 y 24, T4244 1632, www.punta delestehostel.com. Central and basic, US\$17-40 in dorm (also has some doubles), lockers, free internet useage, book exchange, city maps provided.

Maldonado eastern beaches *p65*
San Rafael (Parada 12)
\$\$\$\$ La Capilla, Viña del Mar y Valparaíso, behind San Marcos, T4248 4059, www.lacapilla.com.uy. Open all year. **\$\$\$** in low season, kitchenette in some rooms, safes in rooms, gardens, pool, good.

$$$$-$$$ San Rafael, Lorenzo Batlle y Pacheco, Parada 11, Playa Brava, T4248 2161, www.hotelsanrafael. com.uy. Open all year. Large hotel, heating, safe, spa. Business and events facilities.

La Barra and around p65

$$$$ Hostal de la Barra, Ruta 10, Km 161, T4277 1521, www. hostaldelabarra.net. Open all year. In low season prices drop to **$$$**. A small, neat hotel, not a hostel, with sea view, forest view and loft rooms. Christmas, Carnival and Semana Santa require 7- or 4-night minimum stays.

$$$$ Kalá, Pedregal s/n, Altos de Montoya, T4277 3500, www.kala hotel.com. A boutique hotel with 12 rooms, with breakfast, bars, pools and jacuzzi, bicycles.

$$$$ La Posta del Cangrejo, hotel/ restaurant, Ruta 10, Km 160, T4277 0021, www.lapostadelcangrejo.com. Nice location, smart, prices reduced in low season. Recommended.

$$$$ Mantra, Ruta 10, Parada 48, T4277 1000, www.mantraresort.com. Open all year. Very good and award-winning, but you will need a car to move around, great pool, spa, casino, restaurants, concerts, own cinema and wine bar.

$$-$ pp Backpacker de La Barra, Calle 9, No 2306, 0.5 km off main road, T4277 2272, www.backpackerdela barra.com. Youth-hostel style, price depends on dates and class of room (**$$$$** in luxury double, high season), café, pool, gardens, laundry, bike hire, breakfast included.

$$-$ pp El Viajero Manantiales Beach Hostel, Manantiales, Ruta 10, Km 164, T4277 4427, www. elviajerohostels.com. Private and shared dorms, swimming pool, open-air bar, barbecue area and terrace, breakfast included, free Wi-Fi.

Camping

Camping San Rafael, Camino Aparicio Saravia, T4248 6715, www.campingsanrafael.com.uy. Good facilities, US$8.50-12.50 for 2, also has *cabañas*, Wi-Fi, bus No 5 from Maldonado.

José Ignacio p65

$$$$ Estancia Vik, Camino Eugenio Saiz Martínez, Km 8, José Ignacio, T9460 5212, www.vikretreats.com. Also owned by the Vik family, this impeccable haven of laid-back luxury offers one of the finest estancia stays in Uruguay. Excellent green credentials, extensive views across the José Ignacio Lagoon, exquisite *asados*, modern and traditional art in the rooms and suites. Horse riding and other activities offered. Highly recommended.

$$$$ Playa Vik, C Los Cisnes, T4486 2611/19, www.vikretreats.com. 6 luxurious beach houses, as well as accommodation in the main building, the Pavilion, all overlooking the sea and gardens. Fabulous modern art throughout the property, infinity pool, gym, spa and barbecue dining room. Also **Bahía Vik** (www.vikretreats.com), set to open autumn 2014.

$$$$ Posada del Faro, C de la Bahía y Timonel, T4486 2110, www.

posadadelfaro.com. Exclusive hotel overlooking the sea, 12 rooms in 3 standards, pool, bar, restaurant.

Pueblo Garzón p66
$$$$ Laguna Garzón Lodge, Ruta 10, Km 190.5, T4480 6016, www. lagunagarzon.com.uy. Open year-round subject to weather conditions. This unusual boutique hotel offers 12 rooms, floating on Laguna Garzón. Personalized service, boat trips on the lagoon, birdwatching and trekking.

La Paloma and around p66
$$$$-$$$ Palma de Mallorca, on Playa La Aguada, in nearby La Aguada, T4479 6739, www.hotelpalmade mallorca.com. Right on the ocean. Discounts for longer stays, heated pool, parking.
$$$ Bahía, Av del Navío s/n, entre Solari y Del Sol, T4479 6029, www.el bahia.com.uy. Breakfast, double or triple rooms, clean and simple, quite old-fashioned, laundry, half-board available.

Youth hostels
$ pp Altena 5000 at Parque Andresito, T4479 6396. HI discounts, 50 beds in 4 rooms, good meals, kitchen, open all year.
$ pp Ibirapitá, Av Paloma s/n, near bus station and beach, T4479 9303, www.hostelibirapita.com. Open year-round. Cheaper in mixed dorm and for HI members, doubles **$$**. Buffet breakfast, surf boards, bicycles.

Camping
Parque Andresito, ruta 15, Km 1500, T4479 6081, complejoandresito@

adinet.com.uy. Overpriced, thatched *cabañas* for rent, from US$52 per day with maid and kitchen facilities, sleep 4-6. **Grill del Camping** for *parrillas*.

Barra de Valizas and around p67
At **Cabo Polonio** you cannot camp. There are posadas, some listed below, or you can rent a house; see **www.cabopolonio.com** or **www. portaldelcabo.com.uy** for all options. Water is drawn from wells (*cachimbas*) and there is no electricity (some houses have generators, some gas lamps, otherwise buy candles). There are 4 shops for supplies, the largest is **El Templao**.
$$$ La Perla, Cabo Polonio, T4470 5125, www.laperladelcabo.com. Open all year. Restaurant and snack bar, spa, visits to lighthouse.
$$$ Posada Mariemar, Cabo Polonio, T4470 5164, 9987 5260, mariemar@ cabopolonio.com. Open all year. Nice owners, own electricity generator, hot water, with breakfast, restaurant.
$$$ Posada Valizas, C Tomás Cambre, 1 block from Plaza de los Barcos, Barra de Valizas, T4475 4067, www. posadavalizas.com. Tranquil and lovely, small-scale posada. Peaceful garden setting, friendly and attentive service. Highly recommended.
$$$ Pueblo Barrancas, Ruta 10, Km 227.5, T4479 2236, www. pueblobarrancas.com. Glamping, gastronomy and *cabañas* with a focus on eco and responsible tourism.
$$$-$$ La Pedrasanta, C Cabo Polonio (Cedrón), La Pedrera, T4479 2179, www.posadalapedrasanta. com. Lovely, arty Italian/Argentinean-

run posada and restaurant. Pleasant garden, Tuscan cuisine, friendly owners. Recommended.

$$-$ pp Cabo Polonio Hostel, T9944 5943, www.cabopoloniohostel.com. Small wooden hostel, hot showers, shared rooms, doubles available outside high season, kitchenettes, solar power, bar, good fresh food, can arrange tours and riding.

$$-$ pp Reserva Ecológica La Laguna, 2 km north of Aguas Dulces, T4475 2118/9960 2410. Rustic cabins on the shore a lake, also hostel lodging, day rates for adults and children, full- and half-board available, close to beach, horse riding, trekking, sailing, hydrobikes, meditation. Always phone in advance for directions and reservation.

Youth hostels

$$$-$$ Hostel Valizas, Aladino Veiga s/n, T4475 4045, hostelvalizas@hotmail.com. LGBT-run hostel with dorms and doubles, a short walk from the beach. Large and excellent cooking facilities, barbecue, common rooms, laundry service. HI-affiliated.

$$-$ Lucky Valizas hostel and camping, C Tomás Cambre casa 115, esq Artigas Acosta, T4475 4070, www.luckyvalizas.com. Open year-round. One of the most established and popular hostels. Doubles, set in cute *cabañas*, and dorms sleeping up to 16 people, bathrooms separate for all types of accommodation. Breakfast included, small bar, large outdoor *asado* area. Very spacious, close to nature, friendly staff. Recommended.

$ pp El Viajero La Pedrera Hostel and Suites, C Venteveo s/n, La Pedrera, T4479 2252, www.elviajerohostels.com. Private en suite, dorms en suite, breakfast included, bar, wide common areas, gorgeous garden, free Wi-Fi.

Camping

Camping PP, Ruta 10, Km 226.5, T4479 2069, La Pedrera, www.campingpp.com.uy. US$7.50-11.50 camping, also has cabins for 2 to 6 people.

Punta del Diablo *p68*

In high season you should book in advance; www.portaldeldiablo.com gives a full list of choices.

$$$$ Aquarella, Av No 5, ½ block from beach, T4477 2400, www.hotelaquarella.com. Pool, jacuzzi, great views, gourmet restaurant.

$$$$-$$$ Terrazas de la Viuda, C del Indio, T9968 1138, www.terrazasdelaviuda.com. Pleasant hotel with spacious rooms and pool, overlooking the beach. Balconies with sea view, beach towels provided, some rooms with jacuzzi, breakfast included. Also nearby sister hotel **La Viuda del Diablo** (www.laviudadeldiablo.com), on the beach itself, with restaurant and beach bar open to the public. Good, fresh seafood. Recommended.

$$$-$$ Hostería del Pescador, on road into village, Blv Santa Teresa, T4477 2017, www.portaldeldiablo.com. Rooms for 2-6, prices vary for season and day of week, restaurant, pool.

$$ Hostel and bar Pueblo Arriba, Calles 9 and 16, T4477 2279, www.puebloarriba.com. 4 blocks north of Playa del Rivero lies what's essentially a village within the village. Pueblo Arriba is both a rambling hostel and an art/music space with a bar open to the public, hosting art exhibitions and more. Part of a network of LGBT-friendly hostels.

$$-$ Unplugged Hostel, Calle 10, www.unpluggedhostel.com. Dorm-only hostel not far from the beach, Friendly, sociable place, outdoor communal area for *asados* and pizzas, free computer, good place to meet other travellers.

$$-$ Vente al Diablo Hostel, near Playa de la Viuda, T4477 2691, www. portaldeldiablo.com.uy. 'Come to the Devil' is a rather friendly shack near the beach with an alternative vibe – yoga classes, organic garden and just a few metres from the sea.

$ pp **El Diablo Tranquilo Hostel and Bar**, Av Central, T4477 2647, www. eldiablotranquilo.com. Shared and private rooms, breakfast and cooking facilities, year-round. Separate bar that is one of the nightlife hotspots. Highly recommended. Also **El Diablo Tranquilo Playa Suites** on the beach, run by the same team (double suites with fireplaces (**$$$-$$**).

$ pp **Punta del Diablo Hostel**, Km 298, Ruta 9 parada 2, T4477 2655, www.puntadeldiablohostel.com. Mid-Dec to end Feb. Discounts for HI members. With kitchen, camping (US$8-10 per person), bicycles.

Camping
Camping de la Viuda ($), near Playa de la Viuda, 700 m from the bus station (signposted from there), T4477 2228, www.campingdela viuda.com. Unusually, this campsite is open year-round. Well-equipped with free Wi-Fi, volleyball pitch, shop, laundry service and more. Also, on the way out of town, **Camping Punta del Diablo ($$-$)**.

Parque Nacional Santa Teresa
p69, map p70
La Coronilla
$$$$ Hotel Parque Oceánico, Ruta 9, Km 312.5, T4476 2883, www. hotelparqueoceanico.com.uy. Open year-round. 4-star hotel in excellent location. 3 pools, 1 indoor, 2 outdoor, games room, full- and half-board options. Good restaurant also open to the public. Extensive grounds, short walk to endless beaches. Hiking, birdwatching, horse riding on the beach, forest walks. Highly recommended.

Chuy *p71*
All hotels are open year-round.
$$$ Parador El Fortín de San Miguel, Paraje 18 de Julio, near San Miguel fortress, T4474 6607, www. elfortin.com. Excellent, full and half-board available, Spanish colonial-style hotel built in 1945. Beautiful rooms, gym, 2 pools, restaurant, extensive garden. Friendly, recommended.
$$$-$$ Nuevo Hotel Plaza, Av Artigas y C Arachanes, T4474 2309, www.hotelplaza.chuynet.com. On the plaza, with bath, good buffet breakfast, very helpful, restaurant **El Mesón del Plaza**.
$$ Alerces, Laguna de Castillos 578, T4474 2260, hotelalerceschuy@adinet. com.uy. 4 blocks from border. Bath, breakfast, heater, pool.

$$ Victoria, Numancia 143, T4474 3547. Price includes breakfast, simple and clean, parking.

Camping

From Chuy buses run every 2 hrs to the **Complejo Turístico Chuy** campsite, Ruta 9, Km 331, turn right 13 km, T4474 9425, www.complejo turisticochuy.com. Good bathing, many birds. *Cabañas* and *hostal* accommodation for 2 people or more start at **$$$**, depending on amenities, camping from US$12.50 per person.

❶ Restaurants

Portezuelo and Punta Ballena
p61

$$$ Medio y Medio, Continuación Camino Lussich s/n, Punta Ballena, T4257 8791, www.medioymedio.com. Jazz club and restaurant, music nightly and good food.

$$$-$$ Las Vertientes, Camino de Los Ceibos, 2 km on the Route 9, T4266 9997, www.lasvertientes.com.uy. Country restaurant, fresh food which all comes from own farm, good salads and sweets.

Maldonado *p62*

$$$-$$ Lo de Rubén, Santa Teresa 846 y Florida, T4222 3059, www. loderuben.com.uy. Open every day. *Parrillada*, best restaurant in town.

$$$-$$ Taberna Patxi, Dodera 944, T4223 8393. Very good Basque food with authentic recipes.

Punta del Este *p62, map p63*
Numerous enticing ice cream parlours on Gorlero. There are many more excellent restaurants beyond the peninsula.

$$$ Gure-etxe (also in La Coronilla), Calle 9 y Calle 12, T4244 6858. Seafood and Basque cuisine.

$$$ Isidora, Rambla Artigas, esq 21, T4244 9646, www.isidora.com.uy. Smart, by the port, international cuisine beautifully presented.

$$$ La Bourgogne, Pedragosa Sierra y Av del Mar, T4248 2007, www.relais chateaux.com. Head chef Jean-Paul Bondoux recreates authentic Burgundy cuisine at this **Relais & Chateaux** property near Punta del Este. Exquisite gourmet dining, beautiful surroundings.

$$$ Lo de Charlie, Calle 12 y Calle 9, T4244 4183. Fish, including tuna and octopus, plus pasta and *parrilla* standards.

$$$ Lo de Tere, Rambla Artigas y 21, T4244 0492, www.lode tere.com. Good local food, open all year but closed Wed in winter, 20% discount if eating lunch before 1300 or dinner before 2100. Highly recommended.

$$$ Los Caracoles, Calle 20 y 28, T4244 0912. Excellent food (international, *parrilla*, seafood) at good prices.

$$$ Viejo Marino, Calle 11 entre 14 y 12, Las Palmeras, T4244 3565. Fish restaurant, busy, go early.

$$$ Yatch Club Uruguayo, Rambla Artigas y 8, T4244 1056, www.ycu.org. uy. Very good, fish, seafood, views over the port (not to be confused with the Yacht Club, Calle 10 y 13, which has an expensive restaurant).

$$ Il Barreto, Calle 9 y 10, T4244 5565. Open daily year-round. Italian vegetarian, good value.

La Barra and around p65
$$$ Baby Gouda Deli Café, Ruta 10, Km 161, T4277 1874. Alternative food, yoga and Arab dances.
$$$-$$ Restaurant T, Ruta 10, Km 49.5, T4277 1356. Old-style, Italian and French as well as local dishes, good wine selection. Claims to be the only 'real' bistro in Punta del Este.

Manantiales
$$$ Cactus y Pescados, Primera Bajada a Playa Bikini y Ruta 10, T4277 4782. Very good seafood, international menu.
$$$ El Abrazo, Ruta 10, Km 164.5, T4277 4140, www.elabrazorestaurant. com. Uruguayan dishes with interesting international twists, local produce used, including fresh seafood and olive oil from nearby Colinas de Garzón.

José Ignacio p65
$$$ La Huella, Los Cisnes on Playa Brava, T4486 2279, www.parador lahuella.com. Excellent seafood, on the beach.
$$$ La Susana, Ruta 10, Km 182.5, T4486 2823, www.lasusana.com. A new addition to José Ignacio's food scene, **La Susana** is a beach club, bar and eatery during the day and gourmet restaurant at night. Fabulous location right on the beach for sunset cocktails (excellent range). Delicious, easy-going international cuisine. Recommended.

$$$ Marismo, Ruta 10, Km 185, T4486 2273. Romantic, outdoor tables around a fire.
$$$-$$ La Olada, Ruta 10, Km 181.5, T4486 2745. Intimate, family-run restaurant, clay-oven cooked food. Pleasant.
Mutate, Las Garzas, in front of the main square. Friendly café and shop with a varied cake menu and home-made muffins.

Pueblo Garzón p66
$$$ Restaurante Garzón, Ruta 9, Km 175, T4410 2811, www.restaurante garzon.com. Sizzling dishes cooked Andean style in wood-fire ovens and with iron griddles. Wide variety of dishes, fine dining, wines from their own vineyards.

La Paloma p66
$$$ La Marea, Av Solari y Av Paloma, near tourist office, T4479 7456. Very popular, has outstanding seafood.
$$ Arrecife, Av Solari y C de la Virgen, T4479 6837. First class, serving pizzas, *parrilla* and a good range of salads.
$$ Da Carlis, Av Solari, T4479 7873. Moderate prices, pizzas plus Uruguayan food.

Barra de Valizas and around p67
Barra de Valizas has several restaurants along C Principal, including **Hipocampo ($$)**, specializing in wok dishes, **El Cholo ($$)**, the best established pizza place, and several food shops known as '*auto servicios*'. C Principal ends in the main square, Plaza Leopoldina, home to **La Fraterna ($$)**, a cooperatively run restaurant

with fresh seafood, home-made pastas and ice cream. Further down, on the beach itself is **La Proa** (**$$**), laid-back and serving excellent seafood, paellas and smaller tapas-style dishes. Off the square you'll find **Punto G** (**$**), an excellent ice cream parlour which also offers tourist info and free computer use for guests.

Cabo Polonia

In Cabo Polonio, there are a few restaurants, some with vegetarian options, so you don't have to bring any food with you. Fish is on the menu when the sea is calm enough for the fishermen to go out. The most expensive and fashionable is **La Puesta** (**$$$**), on the south beach. At weekends during the summer there are DJs, dancing and live music. For self-catering, the stores sell fruit, vegetables, meat, etc.

Castillos

There are several restaurants in Castillos including **La Strada** (**$$$**), on 19 de Abril.

Punta del Diablo *p68*

Restaurants in Punta del Diablo, although still fairly ramshackle in appearance, have improved in quality. In main street San Martín, **El Timón** (**$$-$**) does very good pizzas and there are a number of stalls/shacks selling *empanadas* and seafood. Down towards the seafront try **Mirácolo** for wood-fired pizzas, and **Lo de Olga** for meat and fish dishes. There is also **Mandala Mandela** for more

Uruguayan dishes and a Mexican restaurant next door. Opposite **Playa del Pescador**, the *pescadores* themselves sell the catch of the day. **$$ Chivito Veloz**, Aguas Dulces. Good, large portions for US$5.

Parque Nacional Santa Teresa
p69, map p70

$$ La Ruta, L Fernández Tunón, La Coronilla, T4476 2788. Small round restaurant at the entrance to town serving good meat dishes. Most restaurants in La Coronilla and around are closed in the low season, so this may be your only option if you are driving from Chuy to Punta or Montevideo (especially in the evening).

Chuy *p71*

$$-$ Fusion, Av Brasil 387 y Numancia. Good food, traditional Uruguayan fare and pizzas. Recommended
$$-$ Restaurant Jesús, Av Brasil 603 y L Olivera. Good value and quality.

⭘ Bars and clubs

Punta del Este *p62, map p63*
Hop, Rambla Artigas y Calle 12, T4244 6061. Bar and restaurant, popular drinking spot.
Moby Dick, Rambla Artigas 650, T4244 1240, www.mobydick.com.uy. Mock English-style pub by the port, open until the early hours, very popular.
Ocean Club, Parada 12 de la Playa Brava, T4248 4869. Very fashionable and smart club playing mostly pop and house. Dress up.

⏱ What to do

Cabalgatas Valiceras, C Tomás
Cambre s/n, Barra de Valizas, T099 574
685, www.cabalgatasvaliceras.com.uy
(also booked through Lares, see
Montevideo, page 34). Experienced,
responsible tour operator, organizes
longer and shorter horse-riding tours
with an emphasis on culture, nature,
history, flora and fauna. They offer
4 different shorter tours, full- or half-
day (US$80-60) including Valizas to
Cabo Polonio and to La Laguna near
Aguas Dulces. Open between Dec
and Apr when they also do a monthly
full-moon ride with champagne and
dinner on the beach. Recommended
for absolute beginners right through
to experienced riders. 3-, 5- or 7-day
rides also organized.
El Anastacio active tours, Laguna
Anastacio, Ruta 9, Km 143.5, José
Ignacio, T4410 2093. Kite-surfing
classes on the Laguna Anastacio, also
canoeing and horse-riding tours.
Kite- and wind-surfing school, Laguna
Garzón, T4486 20 60 (Dec-Feb only).

⏚ Transport

Piriápolis *p61*
Piriápolis may be reached either by
following the very beautiful R10 from
the end of the Interbalnearia, or by
taking the original access road (R37)
from Pan de Azúcar, which crosses the
R93. The shortest route from Piriápolis
to Punta del Este is by the Camino de
las Bases which runs parallel to the
R37 and joins the R93 some 4 km east
of the R37 junction.

Bus
Terminal on Misiones, 2 blocks from
Hotel Argentino, T4432 4141. To/
from **Montevideo**, US$6.50, 1½ hrs.
To **Punta del Este**, US$6, 50 mins.
To **Maldonado**, US$5, 40 mins. For
Rocha, **La Paloma** and **Chuy**, take
bus to Pan de Azúcar and change.

Maldonado *p62*
Bus
Av Roosevelt y Sarandí, T4222 9300.
To/from **Montevideo**, 2 hrs, US$9;
to **Minas**, 2 hrs, 6 a day, US$6. To **San
Carlos** take a local bus 3 blocks from
the main bus station, US$2.50.

Punta del Este *p62, map p63*
Air
Direct daily Boeing 737 flights from
Buenos Aires to the new Punta del
Este airport during the high season.
Capitán Curbelo (formerly Laguna del
Sauce, T4255 9777), which handles
flights to Buenos Aires, 40 mins.
Airport tax US$31. Exchange facilities,
tax-free shopping. Regular bus service
to airport from Punta del Este (will
deliver to and collect from private
addresses and hotels), US$5, 90 mins
before departure, also connects
with arriving flights. Taxi US$30-40;
remise around US$35 depending on
destination (T4255 9100). **El Jagüel**
airport is used by private planes.

Bus
Local Traffic is directed by a one-way
system; town bus services start from
Calle 5 (El Faro), near the lighthouse.

Long distance Terminal at Av Gorlero, Blv Artigas and Calle 32, T4248 6810 (served by local bus No 7); has toilets, newsagent, café, free luggage storage and casa de cambio. To/from **Montevideo** via Carrasco airport, **COT** (T4248 6810), US$9, just over 2 hrs, many in the summer; at least hourly in winter. To **Piriápolis**, US$6. To **San Carlos** (US$2.50) for connections to Porto Alegre, Rocha, La Paloma, Chuy. Direct to **Chuy**, 4 hrs, US$18. Local bus fare about US$1. For transport Montevideo–Buenos Aires, **Buquebus** T130, at bus terminal, local 09, buses connect with ferries. Also **Colonia Express** and **Seacat**.

The hop-on, hop-off **Summerbus** (www.summerbus.com, see Montevideo Transport, page 38) also stops in Punta del Este and many other parts of the coast.

Car and scooter hire
Punta Car, Artigas 101 y Risso, T4248 2112, www.puntacar.com.uy. And others.
Filibusteros, Av Artigas y Parada 5, T4248 4125. Scooters hire at US$51 per day, with driver's licence (US$50 fine if caught without it) and ID documents. They also rent out bicycles (US$3.50 per hr, US$7.50 per half day, US$10 per day, includes padlocks).

La Paloma *p66*
Bike rental
El Tobo, T4479 7881. US$3.50 a day.

Bus
Frequent to and from **Rocha**, US$2.65, and to and from **Montevideo** (5 hrs,

US$15.50). 4 buses daily to **Chuy**, US$12, 3½ hrs, 2 a day to San Carlos, Pan de Azúcar and Aguas Dulces, all with **Rutas del Sol**, www.rutasdelsol. com.uy. Northeast of La Paloma, some Montevideo–Chuy buses go into **Punta del Diablo**, 4 km from the main road (taxi to the centre US$5.50, 'golf cart taxi' much cheaper at US$1.10).

To **Cabo Polonio**, Rutas del Sol from Montevideo, US$20, 4-5 hrs, and any of the coastal towns to Km 264, where you catch the truck for the village (see above).

Chuy *p71*
Bus
To **Montevideo** (COT, Cynsa, Rutas del Sol) US$23-25, 4¾-6 hrs, you may have to change buses in San Carlos; to **Maldonado** US$11. International buses passing through en route from Montevideo to Brazil either stop in Chuy or at the border. Make sure the driver knows you need to stop at Uruguayan immigration. Sometimes everybody must get off for customs check. If looking for onward transport and there is a free seat, most companies will let you pay on board.

---

❶ Directory

Punta del Este *p62, map p63*
Banks Best rates of exchange from BROU, which opens earlier and closes later than the other banks and accepts MasterCard, but no TCs. Many ATMs at banks on the peninsula and at Punta Shopping (Roosevelt). Also casas de cambio, eg **Indumex**, Av Roosevelt parada 6, **Brimar**, Calle 31 No 610.

La Paloma *p66*
Bank 1 bank which changes TCs. **Other services** Internet, a supermarket and post office.

Chuy *p71*
Banks Several casas de cambios on Av Brasil, eg **Gales**, Artigas y Brasil, Mon-Fri 0830-1200, 1330-1800, Sat 0830-1200, and in World Trade Center, open 1000-2200; on either side of Gales are Aces and Val. All give similar rates, charging US$1 plus 1% commission on TCs, US$, pesos and reais. On Sun, try the casino, or look for someone on the street outside the casas de cambios. No problem spending reais in Chuy or pesos in Chuí. ATMs on the coast can be found in Paseo del Rivero in Punta del Diablo, Santa Teresa national park, La Coronilla, Castillos and Chuy.

Montevideo north to Brazil

Two roads run towards Melo, heart of cattle-ranching country: Route 8 and Route 7, the latter running for most of its length through the Cuchilla Grande, a range of hills with fine views. Route 8 via Minas and Treinta y Tres is the more important of these two roads to the border and it is paved all the way.

Minas and around → *Population: 39,909. For listings, see pages 87-89.*

This picturesque small town, 120 km north of Montevideo, is set in wooded hills. Juan Lavalleja, the leader of the Thirty-Three who brought Independence to the country, was born here, and there is an equestrian statue to Artigas, said to be the largest such statue in the world, on the **Cerro Artigas** just out of town. The church's portico and towers are worth seeing, as are some caves in the neighbourhood and the surrounding countryside. Good confectionery is made in Minas; you can visit the largest firm, opposite Hotel Verdun. Banks are open Monday to Friday 1300-1700. There is a **tourist office** at the bus station. See www.lavalleja.gub.uy and www.destinominas.com.uy.

The **Parque Salus**, on the slopes of Sierras de las Animas, is 8 km to the south and very attractive; take the town bus marked 'Cervecería Salus' from plaza to the Salus brewery, then walk 2 km to the mineral spring and bottling plant (see **Parador Salus**, page 87). It is a lovely three-hour walk back to Minas from the springs. The **Cascada de Agua del Penitente**, 11 km east off Route 8, is an interesting waterfall and you may see wild rheas nearby. It's hard to get to off season. The Minas area is popular for mountain biking.

To the Brazilian border → *For listings, see pages 87-89.*

Route 8 continues north via **Treinta y Tres** (population 27,304) to Melo (also reached by Route 7), near Aceguá close to the border. In **Melo** (population 54,674), there are places to stay and exchange rates are usually better than at the frontier. If crossing to Brazil here, Brazilian immigration is at Bagé, not at the border. At 12 km southeast of Melo is the Posta del Chuy (2 km off Route 26). This house, bridge and toll gate (built 1851) was once the only safe crossing place on the main road between Uruguay and Brazil. It displays gaucho paintings and historical artefacts.

Río Branco was founded in 1914, on the Río Yaguarón. The 1-km-long Mauá bridge across the river leads to Jaguarão in Brazil. The Brazilian vice-consulate in Río Branco is at 10 de Junio 379, T4675 2003, bravcrb@gmail.com, Monday-Friday 0800-1200 and 1400-1800. For road traffic, the frontier at Chuy is better than Río Branco or Aceguá. There is a toll 68 km north of Montevideo.

Also in the area is **Quebrada de los Cuervos national park** ① *Ruta 8, Km 306.7, T4452 2911 (visitor centre), www.snap.gub.uy*, with scenic hiking trails amidst waterfalls and stunning ravines.

An alternative route to Brazil is via Route 5, the 509-km road from Montevideo to the border town of Rivera, which runs almost due north, bypassing Canelones and Florida before passing through Durazno. After crossing the Río Negro, it goes to Tacuarembó. South of the Río Negro is gently rolling cattle country, vineyards, orchards, orange, lemon and olive groves. North is hilly countryside with steep river valleys and cattle ranching. The road is dual carriageway as far as Canelones.

East of Florida, Route 56 traverses the countryside eastwards to **Cerro Colorado**, also known as Alejandro Gallinal, which has an unusual clock tower.

Durazno → *Population: 35,862.*

On the Río Yí 182 km from Montevideo, Durazno is a friendly provincial town with tree-lined avenues and an airport. There is a good view of the river from the western bridge. See http://durazno.gub.uy.

Dams on the Río Negro have created an extensive network of lakes near **Paso de los Toros** (population 14,205), 66 km north of Durazno (bus from Montevideo, 3½ hours, US$16.50), with camping and sports facilities. Some 43 km north of Paso de los Toros a 55-km road turns east to **San Gregorio de Polanco**, at the eastern end of Lago Rincón del Bonete. The beach by the lake is excellent, with opportunities for boat trips, horse riding and other sports.

Tacuarembó → *Population: 54,994.*

This is an agro-industrial town and major route centre 390 km north of Montevideo. The nearby Valle Edén has good walking possibilities. Some 23 km west of Tacuarembó, along Route 26, is the **Carlos Gardel Museum** ① *US$1, daily 1000-1700*, a shrine to the great tango singer who was killed in an air crash in Medellín (Colombia). Uruguay, Argentina and France all claim him as a national son. The argument for his birth near here is convincing. There's a large-scale gaucho festival in March/April, www,patriagaucha.com.uy.

Brazilian border

Rivera (population 71,222) is divided by a street from the Brazilian town of Santana do Livramento. Points of interest are the park, the Plaza Internacional, and the dam of Cañapirú. Uruguayan immigration is at the end of Calle Sarandí y Presidente Viera, 14 blocks, 2 km, from the border (take a bus along Agraciada or taxi from bus terminal for around US$2). There is also a tourist office here (T4623 1900). Luggage is inspected when boarding buses out of Rivera; there are also three checkpoints on the road out of town. The Brazilian consulate is at Ceballos 1159, T4622 3278, consbrasrivera@adinet.com.uy. Remember that you must have a Uruguayan exit stamp to enter Brazil and a Brazilian exit stamp to enter Uruguay. In the department of Rivera lies Valle del Lunarejo, a natural protected area of over 20,000 ha, replete with wildlife and pristine landscapes. Hiking tours of the area can be arranged through Lares (see page 34).

⊛Montevideo north to Brazil listings

For hotel and restaurant price codes and other relevant information, see pages 10-12.

⊜ Where to stay

Minas and around *p85*
$$$ Parador Salus, Parque Salus, T4443 1652, www.paradorsalus. com.uy. Good.
$$ Posada Verdun, W Beltrán 715, T4422 4563, www.hotelposadaverdun. com. Good, à la carte restaurant with wood-fire oven on the premises.

Camping
Arequita, Camino Valeriano Magri, T4440 2503. Beautiful surroundings, *cabañas* (for 2 people with shared bathroom US$22), camping US$4.50 each.

To the Brazilian border *p85*
Treinta y Tres
$$$ Pinos de la Quebrada, Ruta 8, Km 316, T095 001 250, www.pinosdela quebrada.com. Authentic estancia a few kilometres from Quebrada de los Cuervos national park. 6 rooms in

a very peaceful setting, horse riding, hiking and river boat trips.
$$ El Capricho, Ruta 8, Km 306.7, T099 267 238. Small estancia near Quebrada de los Cuervos, with 2 well equipped rooms and 2 *cabañas*, sleeping 6.
$$-$ La Posada, Manuel Freire 1564, T4452 1107, www.hotellaposada33. com. With breakfast and Wi-Fi, a good overnight stop.
$ pp Cañada del Brujo, Km 307.5, Ruta 8, Sierra del Yerbal, 34 km north of Treinta y Tres, T4452 2837, T9929 7448, www.pleka.com/delbrujo. Isolated hostel, no electricity, basic but "fantastic", dorm, local food, meals extra, owner Pablo Rado drives you there (US$15), cycling, trekking on foot or horseback, trips to Quebrada de los Cuervos. Recommended.

Melo
$$ Virrey Pedro de Melo, J Muñiz 727, T4642 2673, www.hotelvirrey pedrodemelo.com. Better rooms in new part, 3-star, minibar, Wi-Fi, café.

Cerro Colorado

$$$$ San Pedro de Timote, Km 142, R7, 14 km west of Cerro Colorado, T4310 8086, www.sanpedrode timote.uy. A famous colonial-style estancia, working ranch, landscaped park, 3 pools, cinema, gym, horse riding, good restaurant.

$$$ Arteaga, 7 km off R7 north of Cerro Colorado, T2707 4766, arteaga@ paradaarteaga.com. Typical European estancia, famous, beautiful interior, pool.

Durazno *p86*

There are a few hotels (**$$-$**).

Tourism farm

Estancia Albergue El Silencio, Ruta 14 Km 166, 10 km west of Durazno, T4362 2014 (or T4360 2270, HI member), www.estancia-el-silencio. com. About 15 mins' walk east of bridge over Río Yí where bus stops, clean rooms, riding, swimming, birdwatching. Recommended.

Camping

At 33 Orientales, in a park of the same name by the river, T4362 2806. Nice beach, hot showers, toilets, laundry sinks.

Paso de los Toros

$$-$ Sayonara, Sarandí 302 y Barreto, T4664 2535. 2 blocks from centre, renovated old residence, rooms with bath, a/c and cable TV. Breakfast extra.

San Gregorio de Polanco

$$ Posada Buena Vista, De Las Pitangueras 12, T4369 4841. Overlooking the lake, breakfast extra, snack bar, good, prices rise Dec-Easter.

Tacuarembó *p86*

$$$ Carlos Gardel, Ruta 5, Km 387.500, T4633 0306, www.hotel carlosgardel.com.uy. Internet, pool, restaurant, meeting room.

$$$ Tacuarembó, 18 de Julio 133, T4632 2105, www.tacuarembohotel. com.uy. Breakfast, central, Wi-Fi, safe, restaurant, large pool, parking.

$$ Central, Gral Flores 300, T4632 2841. En suite bathrooms, rooms with or without a/c, laundry service.

$$ pp Panagea, 1 hr from Tacuarembó, T9983 6149, http:// panagea-uruguay.blogspot.com. Estancia and backpackers' hostel, working cattle and sheep farm, home cooking, lots of riding, electricity till 2200 is only concession to modern amenities, many languages spoken.

Camping

Campsites 1 km out of town in the Parque Laguna de las Lavanderas, T4632 4761, and 7 km north on R26 at Balneario Iporá.

Brazilian border: Rivera *p86*

$$$ Uruguay Brasil, Sarandí 440, T4622 3068, www.hoteluruguaybrasil. com.uy. Buffet breakfast, minibar, Wi-Fi area, laundry service, restaurant.

$$$-$$ Casablanca, Agraciada 479, T4622 3221, www.casablanca.com.uy. Comfortable and pleasant.

$$$-$$ Posada del Lunarejo, Ruta 30, Km 238, T4650 6400, www. posadalunarejo.com. Situated close to a nature reserve, offers full- or half-board accommodation, 4WD, horseback or hiking tours of the area and traditional cuisine.

Camping

Municipal site near AFE station, and in the Parque Gran Bretaña 7 km south along R27.

❼ Restaurants

Minas *p85*

Restaurants (**$$**) include **Complejo San Francisco de las Sierras**, Ruta 12, Km 347 (3 km from Minas); **Ki-Joia**, Diego Pérez in front of Plaza Libertad. **Irisarri**, C Treinta y Tres 618. Best pastry shop, *yemas* (egg candy) and *damasquitos* (apricot sweets).

⊖ Transport

Minas *p85*
Bus

To **Montevideo**, US$8, several companies, 2 hrs. To **Maldonado**, US$6, 7 a day, 1½-2 hrs (**COOM**).

To the Brazilian border: Melo
p85
Bus

To **Montevideo** US$28, 5-7 hrs (**Núñez, EGA**). 3 buses daily to **Río Branco**.

Durazno *p86*
Bus

To **Montevideo** US$13, 2½ hrs.

Tacuarembó *p86*
Bus

To/from **Montevideo**, US$26, 4-5 hrs.

Brazilian border: Rivera *p86*
Bus

Terminal at Uruguay y Viera (1.5 km from the terminal in Santa Ana). To/from **Montevideo**, US$35, 5½-7 hrs (**Agencia Central**, **Turil**, **Núñez**). To **Paysandú**, **Copay**, T4622 3733, at 0400, 1600, US$21 To **Tacuarembó**, US$7 (**Núñez, Turil**), no connections for Paysandú. To **Salto**, Mon and Fri 1630, 6 hrs, US$27. For **Artigas**, take bus from Livramento to Quaraí, then cross bridge.

Contents

Buenos Aires & around

Buenos Aires

With its elegant architecture and fashion-conscious inhabitants, Buenos Aires is often seen as more European than South American. Among its fine boulevards, neat plazas, parks, museums and theatres, there are chic shops and superb restaurants. However, the enormous steaks and passionate tango are distinctly Argentine too and to understand the country, you have to know its capital. South and west of Buenos Aires the flat, fertile lands of the *pampa húmeda* stretch seemingly without end, the horizon broken only by a lonely windpump or a line of poplar trees. This is home to the gaucho, whose traditions of music and craftsmanship remain alive.

Arriving in Buenos Aires → *Phone code: 011. Population: Greater Buenos Aires 12.8 million (includes the Federal District and 24 neighbouring districts in the province of Buenos Aires); rest of the province of Buenos Aires 5.7 million (2010 census).*

Orientation

Buenos Aires has two **airports**, **Ezeiza**, for international and few domestic flights, and **Aeroparque**, for domestic flights, most services to Uruguay and some to Brazil and Chile. Ezeiza is 35 km southwest of the centre, while Aeroparque is 4 km north of the city centre on the riverside. All international and interprovincial buses use the Retiro **bus terminal** at Ramos Mejía y Antártida Argentina, which is next to the Retiro **railway station**.

The commercial heart of the city, from Retiro station and Plaza San Martín through Plaza de Mayo to San Telmo, east of Avenida 9 de Julio, can be explored on foot, but you'll probably want to take a couple of days to explore its museums, shops and markets. Many places of interest lie outside this zone, so you will need to use public transport. City **buses** (*colectivos*) are plentiful, see below for city guides, and the **metro**, or Subte, is fast and clean; see Transport, page 123, for fares. Yellow and black **taxis** can be hailed on the street, but if possible, book a radio or a *remise* taxi by phone. Again, see Transport for details. Street numbers start from the dock side rising from east to west, but north/south streets are numbered from Avenida Rivadavia, one block north of Avenida de Mayo rising in both directions. Avenida Roque Sáenz Peña and Avenida Julio A Roca are commonly referred to as Diagonal Norte and Diagonal Sur respectively. ▸▸ *See also Transport, page 123.*

Tourist information

National office ① *Av Santa Fe 883, T4312 2232 or T0800-555 0016, info@ turismo.gov.ar, Mon-Fri 0900-1700*, maps and literature covering the whole country. There are kiosks at Aeroparque and Ezeiza airports, daily 0800-2000.
City information ① *www.turismo.buenosaires.gob.ar, in Spanish only*. There are tourist kiosks open daily downtown at Plaza Roberto Arlt (Esmeralda y Rivadavia), in Recoleta (Avenida Quintana 596, junction with Ortiz), in Puerto Madero (Dock 4, T4315 4265), and at Retiro bus station (ground floor, T4313 0187).

Guided tours are organized by the city authorities, including a Pope Francis tour throughout the city and bike tours in Palermo parks, both on weekends and holidays only: free leaflet from city-run offices and other suggested circuits on city website.

1 Federal District of Buenos Aires

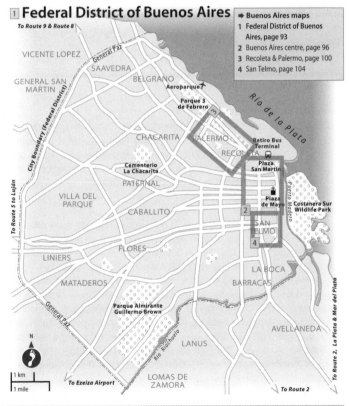

➡ **Buenos Aires maps**
1 Federal District of Buenos Aires, page 93
2 Buenos Aires centre, page 96
3 Recoleta & Palermo, page 100
4 San Telmo, page 104

Those overcharged or cheated can go to the **Defensoría del Turista** ⓘ *Defensa 1250 (San Telmo), T15-2017 6845, turistasantelmo@defensoria.org.ar, Mon-Fri 1000-1800, Sat-Sun and holidays 1100-1800*.

A good guide to bus and subway routes is *Guía T*, available at newsstands. There is also the interactive map at http://mapa.buenosaires.gob.ar. Also handy is Auto Mapa's pocket-size *Plano* of the Federal Capital, US$8.50, or the more detailed *City Map* covering La Boca to Palermo, both available at newsstands, US$3.80; otherwise it is easy to get free maps of the centre from tourist kiosks and most hotels. The daily press has useful supplements, such as the Sunday tourism section in *La Nación* (www.lanacion.com.ar), *Sí* in *Clarín* (www.si.clarin.com) and the equivalent *No* of *Página 12* (www.pagina12.com.ar). The *Buenos Aires Herald* also has information on what's on at www.buenosairesherald.com. For entertainments, see www.agendacultural.buenosaires.gob.ar, www.vuenosairez.com, www.wipe.com.ar and www.whatsupbuenosaires.com. Also very useful are www.gringoinbuenosaires.com and www.discoverbuenosaires.com. Blogs worth exploring include http://baexpats.com and www.goodmorningba.com.

Places in Buenos Aires → *For listings, see pages 107-129.*

The capital has been virtually rebuilt since the beginning of the 20th century and its oldest buildings mostly date from the early 1900s, with some elegant examples from the 1920s and 1930s. The centre has maintained the original layout since its foundation and so the streets are often narrow and mostly one way. Its original name, 'Santa María del Buen Ayre' was a recognition of the favourable winds which brought sailors across the ocean.

Around Plaza de Mayo

The heart of the city is the **Plaza de Mayo**. On the east side is the **Casa de Gobierno**. Called the *Casa Rosada* because it is pink, it contains the offices of the President of the Republic. It is notable for its statuary and the rich furnishing of its halls. The **Museo del Bicentenario** ⓘ *Paseo Colón 100, T4344 3802, www.museobicentenario.gob.ar, Wed-Sun and holidays 1000-1800 Dec-Mar 1100-1900), free*, in the Fuerte de Buenos Aires and Aduana Taylor, covers the period 1810-2010 with historical exhibits and art exhibitions, permanent and temporary. **Antiguo Congreso Nacional** (Old Congress Hall, 1864-1905) ⓘ *Balcarce 139, Thu, 1500-1700, closed Jan-Feb, free*, on the south of the Plaza, is a National Monument. The **Cathedral** ⓘ *San Martín 27, T4331 2845, www.catedralbuenosaires.org.ar, Mon-Fri 0800-1900, Sat-Sun 0900-1930; guided visits to San Martín's Mausoleum and Crypt, religious artefacts, and Temple and Crypt; Mass is held daily, check times*, on the north of Plaza, stands on the site of the first **church** in Buenos Aires. The current structure dates from 1753-1822 (its portico built in 1827), but the 18th-century towers were never rebuilt. The imposing **tomb** (1880) of the Liberator, General José de San Martín (Monday-Saturday 0930-1300, 1500-1700, Sun 0900-1100, 1500-1900), is guarded by soldiers in fancy uniforms. A small exhibition to the left of the main nave displays items related to Pope Francis, former archbishop of Buenos Aires. **Museo del Cabildo y la Revolución de Mayo** ① *Bolívar 65, T4334 1782, www. cabildonacional.gob.ar, Wed-Fri 1030-1700, Sat-Sun and holidays 1130-1800, free*, is in the old Cabildo where the movement for Independence from Spain was first planned. It's worth a visit for the paintings of old Buenos Aires, the documents and maps recording the May 1810 Revolution, and memorabilia of the 1806 British attack; also Jesuit art. In the patio is a café and restaurant and stalls selling handicrafts (Thursday-Friday 1100-1800). Also on the Plaza is the Palacio de Gobierno de la Ciudad (City Hall). Within a few blocks north of the Plaza are the main banks and business houses, such as the **Banco de la Nación**, opposite the Casa Rosada, with an impressively huge main hall and topped by a massive marble dome 50 m in diameter.

On the Plaza de Mayo, the **Mothers of the Plaza de Mayo** march in remembrance of their children who disappeared during the 'dirty war' of the 1970s (their addresses are H Yrigoyen 1584, T4383 0377, www.madres.org, and Piedras 153, T4343 1926, www.madresfundadoras.org.ar). The Mothers march anti-clockwise round the central monument every Thursday at 1530, with photos of their disappeared loved-ones pinned to their chests.

West of Plaza de Mayo
Running west from the Plaza, the Avenida de Mayo leads 1.5 km to the **Palacio del Congreso** (Congress Hall) ① *Plaza del Congreso, Av Rivadavia 1864, T6310 7222 for guided visits, Mon, Tue, Thu, Fri 1000, 1200, 1600, 1800, www.congreso. gov.ar; passport essential*. This huge Greco-Roman building houses the seat of the legislature. Avenida de Mayo has several examples of fine architecture of the early 20th century, such as the sumptuous La Prensa building (No 575, free guided visits at weekends), the traditional **Café Tortoni** (No 825, www. cafetortoni.com.ar), or the eclectic **Palacio Barolo** (No 1370, www.pbarolo. com.ar), and many others of faded grandeur. Avenida de Mayo crosses **Avenida 9 de Julio**, one of the widest avenues in the world, which consists of three major carriageways with heavy traffic, separated in some parts by wide grass borders. Five blocks north of Avenida de Mayo the great **Plaza de la República**, with a 67-m obelisk commemorating the 400th anniversary of the city's founding, is at the junction of Avenida 9 de Julio with Avenidas Roque Sáenz Peña and Corrientes. **Teatro Colón** ① *Cerrito 628, entrance for guided visits Tucumán 1171, T4378 7127, www.teatrocolon.org.ar*, is one of the world's great opera houses. The interior is resplendent with red plush and gilt;

② Buenos Aires centre

To Palermo Parks & Aeroparque

To Recoleta

➡ **Buenos Aires maps**
1 Federal District of Buenos Aires, page 93
2 **Buenos Aires centre, page 96**
3 Recoleta & Palermo, page 100
4 San Telmo, page 104

To La Chacarita Cemetery

To 9

Congreso

Palacio del Congreso

Plaza del Congreso

To 16   To 10

Where to stay

06 Central **1** *D3*
BA Stop **2** *D2*
Bisonte Palace **3** *B3*
Casa Calma **4** *B3*
Castelar **5** *E2*
Colón **6** *C3*
Dolmen **7** *B3*
Dorá **8** *B3*
El Cóndor y el Aguila
  Hostel **9** *D1*
El Conquistador **10** *B3*
Faena Universe **11** *C5*
Goya **12** *C3*
Hispano **14** *D3*
Hostel Suites Obelisco **15** *D3*
Kilca Hostel &
  Backpacker **16** *E1*
La Argentina **17** *E3*
Limehouse **18** *D2*
Marbella **19** *E2*
Milhouse Hostel **20** *E3*
Moreno **21** *E4*
Panamericano &
  Tomo 1 restaurant **23** *C3*
Plaza San Martín Suites **25** *B3*
Portal del Sur **26** *E3*
St Nicholas **27** *D1*
V&S **28** *C3*
Waldorf **29** *B4*

Restaurants 🍴

Al paso y algo más **1** *C4*
Cabaña Las Lilas **2** *D5*
Café Tortoni **3** *D3*
Clásica y Moderna **4** *B1*
Confitería Ideal **5** *D3*
Dadá **6** *B4*
El Gato Negro **7** *C1*
Fikä **8** *E3*
Florida Garden **9** *B4*

Gijón **10** *E2*
Güerrín **11** *D2*
Gianni's **12** *B4/C4*
Las Cuartetas **13** *D3*
Le Grill **14** *D5*
Sam Bucherie **15** *C4*
Sorrento **16** *C4*
Tancat **17** *B3*

Bars & clubs 🍸

Bahrein **18** *C4*
Druid In **19** *B4*
La Cigale **20** *C4*

Museums 🏛

Museo de Armas **2** *B3*
Museo de Arte
  Hispanoamericano
  Isaac Fernández
  Blanco **3** *A3*
Museo de
  la Ciudad **4** *E4*
Museo del
  Bicentenario **5** *E5*
Museo del Cabildo
  y la Revolución
  de Mayo **6** *E4*
Museo del
  Holocausto **7** *B1*
Museo Etnográfico
  JB Ambrosetti **8** *E4*
Museo Judío **9** *C2*
Museo Nacional
  Ferroviario **10** *A3*
Museo y Biblioteca
  Mitre **11** *D4*

the stage is huge and salons, dressing rooms and banquet halls are equally sumptuous. Consult the website for details of performances, tickets and guided visits. Close by is the **Museo Judío** ⓘ *Libertad 769, T4123 0832, www. judaica.org.ar; for visits make an appointment with the rabbi (take identification),* which has religious objects relating to Jewish presence in Argentina in a 19th-century synagogue. Not far away is **Museo del Holocausto** (Shoah Museum) ⓘ *Montevideo 919, T4811 3588, www.museodelholocausto.org.ar, Mon-Thu 1100-1900, Fri 1100-1600, US$1.70 (ID required),* a permanent exhibition of pictures, personal and religious items with texts in Spanish on the Holocaust, antisemitism in Argentina and the lives of many Argentine Jews in the pre- and post-war periods. **La Chacarita** ⓘ *Guzmán 670, daily 0700-1700, take Subte Line B to the Federico Lacroze station.* This well known cemetery has the lovingly tended tomb of Carlos Gardel, the tango singer.

North of Plaza de Mayo

The city's traditional shopping centre, Calle Florida, is reserved for pedestrians, with clothes and souvenir shops, restaurants and the elegant **Galerías Pacífico** ⓘ *Florida entre Córdoba y Viamonte, www.galeriaspacifico.com.ar, guided visits from the fountain on lower ground floor, Mon-Fri, 1130, 1630,* a beautiful mall with fine murals and architecture, many exclusive shops and good food outlets. More shops are to be found on Avenida Santa Fe, which crosses Florida at Plaza San Martín. Avenida Corrientes, a street of theatres, bookshops, restaurants and cafés, and nearby Calle Lavalle (partly reserved for pedestrians), used to be the entertainment centre, but both are now regarded as faded. Recoleta, Palermo and Puerto Madero have become much more fashionable (see below). The **Basílica Nuestra Señora de La Merced** ⓘ *J D Perón y Reconquista 207, Mon-Fri 0800-1800,* founded 1604, rebuilt for the third time in the 18th century, has a beautiful interior with baroque and rococo features. In 1807 it was a command post against the invading British. **Museo y Biblioteca Mitre** ⓘ *San Martín 336, T4394 8240, www.museomitre.gov.ar, Mon-Fri 1300-1730, US$1.70,* preserves intact the household of President Bartolomé Mitre; has a coin and map collection and historical archives.

The **Plaza San Martín** has a monument to San Martín at the western corner of the main park and, at the north end, a memorial with an eternal flame to those who fell in the Falklands/ Malvinas War of 1982. On the plaza is **Palacio San Martín** ⓘ *Arenales 761, T4819 8092, www. mrecic.gov.ar, Thu 1500 free tours in Spanish and English.* Built 1905-1909, it is three houses linked together, now the Foreign Ministry. It has collections of prehispanic and 20th-century art. On the opposite side of the plaza is the opulent **Palacio Paz** (Círculo Militar) ⓘ *Av Santa Fe 750, T4311 1071, www.circulomilitar.org, guided tours Wed-Fri 1100, 1500, Tue 1500, Sat 1100, US$7.50 (in English Wed 1530, US$9,20).* The Círculo Militar includes **Museo de Armas** ⓘ *Av Santa Fe 702, Tue-Fri 1300-1900, Sat*

1400-1900, US$1.70, which has all kinds of weaponry related to Argentine history, including the 1982 Falklands/Malvinas War, plus Oriental weapons.

Plaza Fuerza Aérea Argentina (formerly Plaza Británica) has the clock tower presented by British and Anglo-Argentine residents, while in the **Plaza Canadá** (in front of the Retiro Station) there is a Pacific Northwest Indian totem pole, donated by the Canadian government. Behind Retiro station is **Museo Nacional Ferroviario** ① *Av del Libertador 405, T4318 3343, daily 1030-1800 (closed on holidays), free.* For railway fans: locomotives, machinery, documents of the Argentine system's history; the building is in very poor condition. In a warehouse beside is the workshop of the sculptor Carlos Regazzoni who recycles refuse material from railways.

The **Museo de Arte Hispanoamericano Isaac Fernández Blanco** ① *Suipacha 1422 (3 blocks west of Retiro), T4327 0228, www.museos.buenosaires. gob.ar/mifb.htm, Tue-Fri, 1400-1900, Sat, Sun and holidays 1100-1900, Thu free, US$0.85*, is one of the city's best museums. It contains a fascinating collection of colonial art, especially paintings and silver, also temporary exhibitions of Latin American art, in a beautiful neocolonial mansion (Palacio Noel, 1920s) with Spanish gardens; weekend concerts.

Recoleta and Palermo

Nuestra Señora del Pilar, Junín 1898, is a jewel of colonial architecture dating from 1732 (renovated in later centuries), facing onto the public gardens of Recoleta. A fine wooden image of San Pedro de Alcántara, attributed to the famous 17th-century Spanish sculptor Alonso Cano, is preserved in a side chapel on the left, and there are stunning gold altars. Upstairs is an interesting museum of religious art. Next to it, the **Cemetery of the Recoleta** ① *entrance at Junín 1790, near Museo de Bellas Artes (see below), www. cementeriorecoleta.com.ar, 0700-1700, tours in Spanish and English are available (visitasguiadasrecoleta@buenosaires.gob.ar)*, is one of the sights of Buenos Aires. With its streets and alleys separating family mausoleums built in every imaginable architectural style, La Recoleta is often compared to a miniature city. Among the famous names from Argentine history is Evita Perón who lies in the Duarte family mausoleum: to find it from the entrance go to the first tree-filled plaza; turn left and where this avenue meets a main avenue (go just beyond the Turriaca tomb), turn right; then take the third passage on the left. On Saturday and Sunday there is a good craft market in the park on Plaza Francia outside the cemetery (1000-1800), with street artists and performers. Next to the cemetery, the **Centro Cultural Recoleta** ① *T4803 1040, www. centroculturalrecoleta.org, Tue-Fri 1400-2100, Sat, Sun, holidays 1200-2100*, specializes in contemporary local art.

The excellent **Museo de Bellas Artes** (National Gallery) ① *Av del Libertador 1473, T5288 9999, www.mnba.org.ar, Tue-Fri 1230-2030, Sat-Sun 0930-2030, free,*

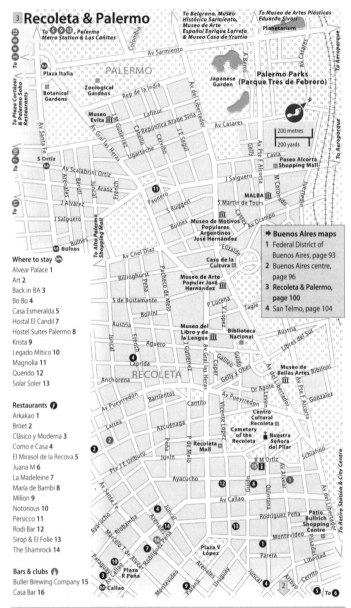

To Belgrano, Museo
Histórico Sarmiento,
Museo de Arte
Español Enrique Larreta
& Museo Casa de Yrurtia

To Museo de Artes Plásticas
Eduardo Sivori

Planetarium

To ⑤⑨⑥⑫, Palermo
Metro Station & Las Cañitas

Colombia

Av Sarmiento

Plaza Italia

PALERMO

Av Casares

To Plaza Cortázar
& Palermo Soho
Restaurants

Botanical
Gardens

Zoological
Gardens

Rep de la India

Japanese
Garden

Palermo Parks
(Parque Tres de Febrero)

Av del Libertador

A Berro

To Aeroparque

Museo
Evita

Lafinur

C.Bello·República Arabe Siria

Av Casares

200 metres

200 yards

To ③⑩

S Ortiz

Av Scalabrini Ortiz

Berutti

Guemes

Av Gral las Heras

Ugarteche

Cerviño

Seguí

Getty

Av Pte A.Alcorta

Cavia

Paseo Alcorta
Shopping Mall

To ⑪

Arenales

J Alvarez

Araoz

French

J Salguero

Paunero

S Ruggeri

J Salguero

MALBA

S Martín de Tours

M Coronado

M Ortiz

To Aeroparque

Bulnes

Av Santa Fe

Bulnes

To Alto Palermo
Shopping Mall

Av Cnel Díaz

Bulnes

Elizalde

Museo de Motivos
Populares
Argentinos
José Hernández

Casey

Av Ocampo

Casa de la
Cultura

Billinghurst

Pacheco de Melo

Peña

Museo de Arte
Popular José
Hernández

P Lucena

V López

Tagle

S de Bustamante

Bollini

P Lucena

Austria

Austria

Museo del
Libro y de
la Lengua

Biblioteca
Nacional

Libert del Sur

Av Gral las Heras

French

Aguero

Guido

Galileo

Coper

Guido

Museo de
Bellas Artes

Bibiloni

Laprida

RECOLETA

Gelly y Obes

Dr Agote

Av del Libertador

Anchorena

Av Pueyrredón

Barrientos

Cantilo

Vicente López

Av Pueyrredón

Dr Agote

Leyes

González

Av Pte A.Alcorta

Larrea

Azcuénaga

Peña

de Melo

Recoleta
Mall

Centro
Cultural
Recoleta

Nuestra
Señora
del Pilar

Schiaffino

To Retiro Station & City Centre

Cemetery
of the
Recoleta

Av Alvear

Junín

R M Ortiz

i

Ayacucho

Pte J E Uriburu

Av Callao

Quintana

Av Callao

Rodríguez Peña

Patio
Bullrich
Shopping
Centre

Juncal

Montevideo

Posadas

Av del Libertador

Plaza V
López

Parera

Av Santa Fe

M.T de Alvear

Paraguay

Riobamba

Arenales

Rodríguez Peña

Juncal

Arenales

Uruguay

Paraná

Libertad

Cerrito

Arroyo

Plaza
R Peña

Callao

To ⑥

To ⑤

Where to stay 🛏
Alvear Palace **1**
Art **2**
Back in BA **3**
Bo Bo **4**
Casa Esmeralda **5**
Hostal El Candil **7**
Hostel Suites Palermo **8**
Krista **9**
Legado Mítico **10**
Magnolia **11**
Querido **12**
Solar Soler **13**

Restaurants 🍴
Arkakao **1**
Bröet **2**
Clásico y Moderna **3**
Como e Casa **4**
El Mirasol de la Recova **5**
Juana M **6**
La Madeleine **7**
María de Bambi **8**
Milion **9**
Notorious **10**
Persicco **11**
Rodi Bar **12**
Sirop & El Folie **13**
The Shamrock **14**

Bars & clubs 🍸
Buller Brewing Company **15**
Casa Bar **16**

➡ **Buenos Aires maps**
1 Federal District of
Buenos Aires, page 93
2 Buenos Aires centre,
page 96
3 Recoleta & Palermo,
page 100
4 San Telmo, page 104

gives a taste of Argentine art, as well as having a fine collection of European works, particularly post-Impressionist. Superb Argentine 19th- and 20th-century paintings, sculpture and wooden carvings; also films, classical music concerts and art courses. **Biblioteca Nacional** (National Library) ① *Av del Libertador 1600 y Agüero 2502, T4808 6000, www.bn.gov.ar, Mon-Fri 0900-2100, Sat and Sun 1200-1900, closed Jan*, is housed in a modern building and contains an art gallery and periodical archives (only a fraction of the extensive stock can be seen); cultural events are held here too. Next to it is the **Museo del Libro y de la Lengua** ① *Av Las Heras 2555, T4808 0090, Tue-Sun 1400-1900, free*, whose exhibitions illustrate singularities of the Spanish (castellano) spoken in Argentina and the local publishing industry. The **Museo Nacional de Arte Decorativo** ① *Av del Libertador 1902, T4802 6606, www.mnad.org.ar, Tue-Sun 1400-1900 (closed Sun in Jan), US$1.70, Tue free, guided visits US$2.50 in Spanish, English and French, check times*, contains collections of painting, furniture, porcelain, crystal and sculpture exhibited in sumptuous halls, once a family residence.

Palermo Chico is a delightful residential area with several houses of once-wealthy families, dating from the early 20th century. The predominant French style of the district was broken in 1929 by the rationalist lines of the **Casa de la Cultura** ① *Rufino de Elizalde 2831, T4808 0553, www.fnartes.gov.ar, Tue-Sun 1500-2000 (Jan closed)*. The original residence of the writer Victoria Ocampo, this was a gathering place for artists and intellectuals and is now an attractive cultural centre with art exhibitions and occasional concerts.

The **Museo de Arte Popular José Hernández** ① *Av del Libertador 2373, T4803 2384, www.museohernandez.buenosaires.gob.ar, Wed-Fri 1300-1900, Sat-Sun and holidays 1000-2000, US$0.20, free Sun; see website for exhibitions, events and workshops*, has a wide collection of Argentine folkloric art, with rooms dedicated to indigenous, colonial and gaucho artefacts; there's a handicraft shop and library. The **Museo de Arte Latinoamericano (MALBA)** ① *Av Figueroa Alcorta 3415, T4808 6500, www.malba.org.ar, Thu-Mon and holidays 1200-2000, US$5.50, students and seniors US$2.75 (Wed half price, students free, open till 2100); Tue closed*, one of the most important museums in the city, houses renowned Latin American artists' works: powerful, moving and highly recommended. It's not a vast collection, but representative of the best from the continent. It also has a good library, cinema (showing art house films as well as Argentine classics), seminars and a shop, as well as an elegant café, serving delicious food and cakes. Of the fine Palermo parks, the largest is **Parque Tres de Febrero**, famous for its extensive rose garden, Andalusian Patio, and the delightful **Jardín Japonés** (with café) ① *T4804 4922, www.jardinjapones.org.ar, daily 1000-1800, US$4, seniors free*. It is a charming place for a walk, delightful for children, and with a good café serving some Japanese dishes. Close by is the **Hipódromo Argentino** (Palermo racecourse) ① *T4778 2800, www.palermo.com.ar, races 10 days per month, free*. Opposite the parks are the Botanical and Zoological Gardens. At the entrance to the **Planetarium** ⓘ *just off Belisario Roldán, in Palermo Park, T4771 6629, www.planetario. gov.ar, 3 presentations Tue-Fri, 5 at weekends, US$4.20; small museum,* are several large meteorites from Campo del Cielo. The **Museo de Artes Plásticas Eduardo Sívori** ⓘ *Av Infanta Isabel 555 (Parque Tres de Febrero), T4774 9452, www.museosivori.org.ar, Tue-Fri 1200-2000, Sat-Sun and holidays 1000-2000 (1800 in winter), US$1.70, Wed free,* emphasises 19th- and 20th-century Argentine art, sculpture and tapestry. The **Botanical Gardens** ⓘ *Santa Fe 3951, T4831 4527, www.jardinbotanico.buenosaires.gob.ar entrance from Plaza Italia (take Subte, line D) or from C República Arabe Siria, Mon-Fri 0800-1800, Sat-Sun 0930-1800 (closes at 1900 in summer), free guided visits Sat-Sun and holidays 1030, 1500,* contain characteristic specimens of the world's vegetation. The trees native to the different provinces of Argentina are brought together in one section; see also the *yerba mate* section. One block beyond is **Museo Evita** ⓘ *Lafinur 2988, T4807 0306, www.museoevita.org, Tue-Sun 1100-1900, US$3.50 for non-residents.* In a former women's shelter run by Fundación Eva Perón, the exhibition of dresses, paintings and other items is quite interesting though lacks the expected passion; there's also a library and a café-restaurant.

In Belgrano is the **Museo de Arte Español Enrique Larreta** ⓘ *Juramento 2291, T4784 4040, Mon-Fri, 1300-1900, Sat-Sun 1000-2000, guided visits Sat-Sun 1600, 1800, US$0.35, Thu free.* The home of the writer Larreta, with paintings and religious art from the 14th to the 20th century, it also has a beautiful garden. See www. mibelgrano.com.ar/museos.htm for two other museums in this district: **Museo Histórico Sarmiento** ⓘ *Juramento 2180, T4782 2354, www.museosarmiento.gov. ar,* and **Museo Casa de Yrurtia** ⓘ *O'Higgins 2390, T4781 0385.*

South of Plaza de Mayo

The church of **San Ignacio de Loyola**, begun 1664, is the oldest colonial building in Buenos Aires (renovated in the 18th and 19th centuries). It stands in a block of Jesuit origin, called the **Manzana de las Luces** (Enlightenment Square – Moreno, Alsina, Perú and Bolívar). Also in this block are the **Colegio Nacional de Buenos Aires** ⓘ *Bolívar 263, T4331 0734,* formerly the site of the Jesuits' Colegio Máximo, the Procuraduría de las Misiones (today the **Mercado de las Luces**, a crafts market) and 18th-century **tunnels**. For centuries the whole block was the centre of intellectual activity, though little remains today but a small **cultural centre** ⓘ *T4343 3260, www.manzanadelasluces.gov.ar, guided tours from Perú 272, Mon-Fri 1500, Sat and Sun 1500, 1630, 1800 in Spanish (in English by prior arrangement), arrive 15 mins before tour, US$2.50; the tours explore the tunnels and visit the buildings on C Perú,* with art courses, concerts, plays and film shows. The **Museo de la Ciudad** ⓘ *Alsina 412, T4343 2123, Mon-Fri 1100-1900, Sat, Sun 1000-2000, US$0.20, free on Mon and Wed,* has a permanent exhibition covering social history and popular culture, and special exhibitions on daily life in Buenos

Aires that are changed every two months. There's also a reference library open to the public.

Santo Domingo ① *Defensa y Belgrano, Mon-Fri 0900-1300, Sun 1000-1200*, was founded in 1751. During the British attack on Buenos Aires in 1806 some of Whitelocke's soldiers took refuge in the church. The local forces bombarded it, the British capitulated and their regimental colours were preserved in the church. General Belgrano is buried here. The church holds occasional concerts.

Museo Etnográfico JB Ambrosetti ① *Moreno 350, T4345 8196, see Facebook, Tue-Fri 1300-1900, Sat-Sun 1500-1900 (closed Jan), US$0.50, guided visits Sat-Sun 1600*. contains anthropological and ethnographic collections from Patagonian and Argentina's northwest cultures (the latter a rich collection displayed on the first floor). There's also a small international room with a magnificent Japanese Buddhist altar.

San Telmo and La Boca

One of the few places which still has late colonial and Rosista buildings (mostly renovated in the 20th century) is the *barrio* of **San Telmo**, south of Plaza de Mayo. It's an atmospheric place, with lots of cafés, antique shops and little art galleries. On Sundays, it has a great atmosphere, with an antiques market at the Plaza Dorrego (see page 121), free tango shows (1000-1800) and live music. The **Museo de Arte Moderno de Buenos Aires (MAMBA)** ① *Av San Juan 350, T4342 3001, Tue-Fri 1100-1900, Sat, Sun and holidays 1100-2000, US$0.85, Tue free*, has temporary art exhibitions from local and foreign artists. Next door is the **Museo de Arte Contemporáneo de Buenos Aires (MACBA)** ① *T5299 2010, www.macba.com.ar, Mon-Fri 1200-1900, Sat, Sun 1100-1930, US$3.50 (Wed US$1.70)*, focusing on geometric abstraction.

East of the Plaza de Mayo, behind the Casa Rosada, a broad avenue, Paseo Colón, runs south towards San Telmo and, as Avenida Almirante Brown, on to the old port district of **La Boca**, where the Riachuelo flows into the Plata. To get there, take a radio taxi from the centre or San Telmo; to return, call for a taxi from any café, US$7 one way. The much-photographed, brightly painted tin and wooden houses cover one block of the pedestrianized Caminito. As La Boca is the poorest and roughest area within central Buenos Aires, tourists are limited to this little street running from the Plaza La Vuelta de Rocha. You can also visit **Fundación Proa** ① *Av Pedro de Mendoza 1929, T4104 1000, www.proa.org, Tue-Sun 1100-1900*, for varied art exhibitions, cultural events and for its café-restaurant with a view, and the **Museo de Bellas Artes Benito Quinquela Martín** ① *Av Pedro de Mendoza 1835, T4301 1080, www.museoquinquela.gov. ar, Tue-Fri 1000-1800, Sat, Sun and holidays 1100-1800 (Tue-Sun 1100-1730 in summer), US$1.70*, with over 1000 works by Argentine artists, particularly Benito Quinquela Martín (1890-1977), who painted La Boca port life. It also houses sculptures and figureheads rescued from ships. Do not go anywhere else in La Boca and avoid it at night. The area is especially rowdy when the Boca Juniors football club is playing at home. At Boca Juniors stadium is **Museo de la Pasión Boquense** ⓘ *Brandsen 805, T4362 1100, www.museoboquense.com, daily 1000-1800, US$9, guided tour of the stadium in Spanish or English, 1100-1700, plus ticket to the museum, US$12.*

Docks and Costanera Sur

Fragata Presidente Sarmiento ⓘ *dock 3, Av Alicia Moreau de Justo 980, Puerto Madero, T4334 9386, daily 1000-1900, US$0.35*, was a naval training ship until 1961; now it's a museum. Nearby, in dock 4, is the **Corbeta Uruguay** ⓘ *T4314 1090, daily 1000-1900, US$0.35, for both ships see www.ara.mil.ar*,

➜ Buenos Aires maps
1. Federal District of Buenos Aires, page 93
2. Buenos Aires centre, page 96
3. Recoleta & Palermo, page 100
4. San Telmo, page 104

Where to stay
Art Factory 1
Axel 2
Circus 3
Garden House 4
Hostal de Granados 5
Hostel-Inn Buenos Aires 6
Kilca Hostel & Backpacker 7
La Casita de San Telmo 8
La Cayetana Historic House 9
Lola House 10
Lugar Gay de Buenos Aires 11
Mansión Dandi Royal 12
Ostinatto 13
Sabatico Travelers Hostel 14
Telmho 16

Restaurants
Brasserie Petanque 1
Británico 2
Dorrego 3
Dylan 4
Gran Parilla del Plata 5
La Brigada 6
La Poesía 7
Naturalisa Sabia 8
Nonna Bianca 9
Pride Café 10

Bars & clubs
Bar Seddon 11

the ship that rescued Otto Nordenskjold's Antarctic expedition in 1903. The **Puerto Madero** dock area has been renovated; the 19th-century warehouses are restaurants and bars, an attractive place for a stroll and popular nightspot. In dock 4 there is also **Colección Fortabat** ⓘ *Olga Cossettini 141, T4310 6600, www.coleccionfortabat.org.ar, Tue-Sun 1200-2000, US$6*, which houses a great art collection. East of San Telmo on the far side of the docks, the Avenida Costanera runs as a long, spacious boulevard. A stretch of marshland reclaimed from the river forms the interesting **Costanera Sur Wildlife Reserve** ⓘ *entrances at Av Tristán Achával Rodríguez 1550 (take Estados Unidos east from San Telmo) or next to the Buquebús ferry terminal (take Av Córdoba east), T4315 4129; for pedestrians and bikers only, Tue-Sun 0800-1800 (in summer, closes at 1900), free,* where over 150 bird species have been spotted over the past few years. Free guided tours at weekends and holidays 0930, 1600, from the administration next to the southern entrance, but much can be seen from the road before then (binoculars useful). Also free nocturnal visits every month on the Friday closest to the full moon (book Monday before, T4313 4275). To get there take colectivos 4, 130 or 152. It's half an hour walk from the entrance to the river shore and about three hours to walk the whole perimeter. In summer it's very hot with little shade. For details (particularly birdwatching) contact **Aves Argentinas/AOP** (see page 129), or see www.reservacostanera.com.ar (English version).

Around Buenos Aires → *For listings, see pages 107-129.*

Tigre → *Population: 42,000 (Partido de Tigre –Tigre county – 376,000).*
This touristy little town, 32 km northwest of Buenos Aires, is a popular weekend destination lying on the lush jungly banks of the Río Luján, with a funfair and an excellent fruit and handicrafts market (Puerto de Frutos, Monday-Friday 1000-1800, Saturday, Sunday and holidays 1000-1900 with access from Calles Sarmiento or Perú). There are restaurants on the waterfront in Tigre across the Río Tigre from the railway line, along Lavalle and Paseo Victorica; cheaper places can be found on Italia and Cazón on the near side, or at the Puerto de Frutos. North of the town is the delta of the Río Paraná: innumerable canals and rivulets, with holiday homes and restaurants on the banks and a fruit-growing centre. The fishing is excellent and the peace is only disturbed by motor-boats at weekends. Regattas are held in November. Take a trip on one of the regular launch services (*lanchas colectivas*) which run to all parts of the delta, including taxi launches – watch prices for these – from the wharf (Estación Fluvial). Tourist catamarans run daily services: one- to two-hour trips, US$13-17, from Lavalle 499 on Río Tigre, T4731 0261/63, www.tigreencatamaran.com.ar, and three to seven services daily, 1½-hour trips,

US$15, from Puerto de Frutos, **Río Tur** (T4731 0280, www.rioturcatamaranes. com.ar). **Sturla** (Estación Fluvial, oficina 10, T4731 1300, www.sturla viajes.com. ar) runs four one-hour trips a day, US$15 (includes a ride on **Bus Turístico**); they also have trips with lunch, night-time boat trips, full-day excursions from the centre of Buenos Aires, commuting services to Puerto Madero, and more. You can also hire kayaks, canoes or rowing boats, rent houses, or visit *recreos*, little resorts with swimming pools, tennis courts, bar and restaurant. **Bus Turístico** (T4731 1300, www.busturisticotigre.com.ar) runs one-hour tours, US$5, every hour on an open-top bus with 10 stops, starting 1040 at the railway station. **Tigre tourist office** ⓘ *by the Estación Fluvial, Mitre 305, T0800-888 84473, www. tigre.gov.ar/turismo, also at Juncal 1600 and the Puerto de Frutos*, with a full list of houses to rent, activities, etc. **Centro de Guías de Tigre y Delta** ⓘ *Estación Fluvial of 2, T4731 3555, www.guiastigreydelta.com.ar*, can organize guided walks and launch trips.

The **Museo Naval** ⓘ *Paseo Victorica 602, T4749 0608, Tue-Fri 0830-1730, Sat-Sun and holidays 1030-1830, US$1.70 (voluntary fee)*, is worth a visit to see the displays on the Argentine navy. There are also relics of the 1982 Falklands/ Malvinas War. The **Museo de Arte** ⓘ *Paseo Victorica 972, T4512 4528, www. mat.gov.ar, Wed-Fri 0900-1900, Sat-Sun 1200-1900, US$2.50*, hosts a collection of Argentine figurative art in the former Tigre Club Casino, a beautiful belle époque building.

Museo del Mate ⓘ *Lavalle 289, T4506 9594, www.elmuseodelmate.com, Wed-Sun 1100-1800 (1100-1900 in summer), US$2.50*, tells the history of *mate* and has an interesting collection of the associated paraphernalia.

Isla Martín García
This island in the Río de la Plata (Juan Díaz de Solís' landfall in 1516) used to be a military base. Now it is an ecological/historical centre and an ideal excursion from the capital, with many trails through the cane brakes, trees and rocky outcrops – interesting birds and flowers. Boat trips: four weekly from Tigre at 0900, returning 2000, three-hour journey, US$55 return including lunch, *asado* and guide; US$90 per person, including weekend overnight at inn, full board. Reservations only through **Cacciola** (address under Tigre, Transport, page 127), who also handle bookings for the inn and restaurant on the island. There is also a campsite.

For hotel and restaurant price codes and other relevant information, see pages 10-12.

◉ Where to stay

Shop around for hotels offering discounts on multi-night stays. The tourist offices at Ezeiza and Aeroparque airports book rooms. A/c is a must in high summer. Finding hotels for Fri, Sat, Sun nights can be difficult and hostels can get very busy, resulting in pressure on staff. A bed in a hostel dorm costs US$10-20. The range of 'boutique' hotels and hostels is impressive, especially in Palermo and San Telmo. The same applies to restaurants, bars and clubs. There are far more than we can list here. There are fine examples of the **Four Seasons** (www.fourseasons. com/buenosaires), **Hilton** (www.hilton. com), **Hyatt** (www.buenosaires.park. hyatt.com), **Marriott** (www.marriott. com), **NH** (www.nh-hoteles.com), **Pestana** (www.pestana.com), **Sofitel** (www.sofitel.com) and **Unique Hotels** (www.uniquehotels.com.ar) chains. Hotels will store luggage, and most have English-speaking staff.

Centre *p94, map p96*
$$$$ Alvear Palace, Av Alvear 1891, T4808 2100, www.alvearpalace.com. The height of elegance, an impeccably preserved 1920s Recoleta palace, sumptuous marble foyer, with Louis XV-style chairs, and a charming orangery where you can take tea with superb patisseries. Antique-filled bedrooms. Recommended.

$$$$ Casa Calma, Suipacha 1015, T5199 2800, www.casacalmahotel. com. A relaxing haven in a downtown setting, homely yet luxurious, with a wellness centre and honesty bar.
$$$$ Faena Universe, Martha Salotti 445 (Puerto Madero), T4010 9000, www.faena.com. Set in a 100-year-old silo, renovated by Philippe Starck, this is not for all budgets or tastes. Eclectic decoration, staff trained to be perfect.
$$$$-$$$ Castelar, Av de Mayo 1152, T4383 5000, www.castelarhotel. com.ar. A wonderfully elegant 1920s hotel which retains all the original features in the grand entrance and bar. Cosy bedrooms, charming staff, and excellent value. Also a spa with Turkish baths and massage. Highly recommended.
$$$$-$$$ Dolmen, Suipacha 1079, T4315 7117, www.hoteldolmen. com.ar. Good location, smart spacious entrance lobby, with a calm relaxing atmosphere, good professional service, modern, comfortable well-designed rooms, small pool.
$$$$-$$$ El Conquistador, Suipacha 948, T4328 3012, www. elconquistador.com.ar. Stylish 1970s hotel, which retains the wood and chrome foyer, but has bright modern rooms, and a lovely light restaurant on the 10th floor with great views. Well situated, good value.
$$$$-$$$ Panamericano, Carlos Pellegrini 551, T4348 5000, www. panamericano.us. Very smart and modern hotel, with luxurious and tasteful rooms, covered rooftop

pool, and superb restaurant, **Tomo 1**. Excellent service too. Also has properties in Bariloche (www. panamericanobariloche.com) and El Calafate (www.casalossauces.com).

$$$ Art, Azcuénaga 1268, T4821 6248, www.arthotel.com.ar. Charming boutique hotel on a quiet residential street, only a few blocks from Recoleta or Av Santa Fe, simply but warmly decorated, good service, solarium, compact standard rooms.

$$$ Bisonte Palace, MT de Alvear 902, T4328 4751, www.hotelesbisonte. com. Charming, with calm entrance foyer, which remains gracious thanks to courteous staff. Plain but spacious rooms, ample breakfast, good location. Very good value.

$$$ Colón, Carlos Pellegrini 507, T4320 3500, www.exehotelcolon.com. Splendid location overlooking Av 9 de Julio and Teatro Colón, extremely good value. Charming bedrooms, comfortable, gym, great breakfasts, and perfect service. Highly recommended.

$$$ Dorá, Maipú 963, T4312 7391, www.dora hotel.com.ar. Charming and old-fashioned with comfortable rooms, good service, attractive lounge with paintings. Warmly recommended.

$$$ Goya, Suipacha 748, T4322 9269, www.goya hotel.com.ar. Welcoming and central, worth paying more for superior rooms, though all are comfortable. Good breakfast, English spoken.

$$$ Hispano, Av de Mayo 861, T4345 2020, www.hhispano.com.ar. Plain but comfortable rooms in this hotel which has been welcoming travellers since the 1950s, courtyard and small garden, central.

$$$ Marbella, Av de Mayo 1261, T4383 3573, www.hotelmarbella. com.ar. Modernized, and central, though quiet, multilingual. Recommended.

$$$ Moreno, Moreno 376, T6091 2000, www.morenobuenosaires.com. 150 m from the Plaza de Mayo, decorated in dark, rich tones, large rooms, good value, jacuzzi, gym and chic bar, winery and restaurant.

$$$ Plaza San Martín Suites, Suipacha 1092, T5093 7000, www. plazasanmartin.com.ar. Neat modern self-contained apartments right in the city centre, comfortable and attractively decorated, with lounge and little kitchen. Pet friendly, room service. Good value.

$$$ Waldorf, Paraguay 450, T4312 2071, www.waldorf-hotel.com.ar. Welcoming staff and a comfortable mixture of traditional and modern in this centrally located hotel. Good value, with a buffet breakfast, English spoken. Recommended.

$ La Argentina, Av de Mayo 860, T4342 0078. Cheap, central and rickety, but it stands the test of time. Amazing old building, bringing new meaning to the term 'high-ceilinged'; can be noisy if your room is near the 'slam-the-door-shut' elevator. Good, cheap and cheerful restaurant attached, doing very affordable *menú del día*. Recommended.

Youth hostels
$ pp 06 Central, Maipú 306, T5219 0052, www.06centralhostel.com.

A few metres from the Obelisco and Av Corrientes, simple, spacious dorms, nicely decorated doubles (**$$**), cosy communal area.

$ pp BA Stop, Rivadavia 1194, T4382 7406, www.bastop.com. In a converted 1900s corner block, dorms, private rooms (**$$** double), large-screen TV, table tennis, bar, English spoken, safe, very helpful staff. Repeatedly recommended.

$ El Cóndor y el Aguila Hostel, Espinosa 1628, near junction Av San Martín and Av Juan B Justo, T4581 6663, www.elcondoryelaguila.com.ar. 5 private rooms and 4 dorms. Terrace, laundry and internet access. Free transfer from Retiro and Aeroparque, and free tea and coffee.

$ pp Hostel Suites Obelisco, Av Corrientes 830, T4328 4040, www. hostelsuites.com. Elegant hostel built in a completely restored old building in the heart of the city. Dorms, doubles and private apartments (**$$**), DVD room, laundry service. Free transfer from Ezeiza airport. HI discount.

$ pp Limehouse Hostel, Lima 11, T4383 4561, www.limehouse.com. ar. Dorms for up to 12 and doubles with and without bath (**$$**), popular, typical city hostel with bar, roof terrace, 'chilled', great if you like the party atmosphere, efficient staff. Recommended.

$ pp Milhouse Hostel, Hipólito Yrigoyen 959, T4345 9604, www. milhousehostel.com. In 1890 house, lovely rooms (**$$$** in double) and dorms, comfortable, laundry, tango lessons, very popular so reconfirm bookings at all times.

$ pp Portal del Sur, Hipólito Yrigoyen 855, T4342 8788, www.portaldelsurba. com.ar. Nice dorms and especially lovely doubles (**$$$**) and singles in a converted 19th-century building. Recommended for single travellers.

$ pp St Nicholas, B Mitre 1691, T4373 5920, www.snhostel.com. Beautifully converted old house, now a party hostel with spotless rooms, large roof terrace and a pub with daily live shows; also double rooms (**$$**).

$ pp V&S, Viamonte 887, T4322 0994, www.hostelclub.com. Central popular hostel (**$$$** in attractive double room, bath), café, tango classes, tours, warm atmosphere, welcoming. Recommended.

Palermo *p99, map p100*

$$$$ Legado Mítico, Gurruchaga 1848, T4833 1300, www.legado mitico.com. Stylish small hotel with 11 rooms named after Argentine cultural legends. They use local designs and products. Luxurious and recommended.

$$$$ Magnolia, Julián Alvarez 1746, T4867 4900, www.magnoliahotel boutique.com. Lovely boutique hotel in a quiet area. This refurbished early 20th-century house has attractively designed rooms opening onto the street or to inner courtyards and a perfect retreat on its rooftop terrace.

$$$$ Querido, Juan Ramírez de Velazco 934, T4854 6297, www. queridobuenosaires.com. Purpose-built, designed and cared for by a Brazilian-English couple. 7 rooms, 4 of which have balconies, for a comfortable stay in Villa Crespo area, a few blocks from Palermo Soho and from the subway.

$$$$-$$$ Bo Bo, Guatemala 4882, T4774 0505, www.bobo hotel.com. On a leafy street, 15 rooms decorated in contemporary style, some with private balconies, excellent restaurant.

$$$$-$$$ Krista, Bonpland 1665, T4771 4697, www.kristahotel.com.ar. Intimate, hidden behind the plain façade of an elegant townhouse, well placed for restaurants. Good value, comfortable, individually designed spacious rooms, wheelchair access.

$$$ Solar Soler, Soler 5676, T4776 3065, www.solarsoler.com.ar. Welcoming B&B in Palermo Hollywood, excellent service. Recommended.

Youth hostels

$ pp Back in BA, El Salvador 5115, T4774 2859, www.backinba.com. Small hostel with dorms for up to 6 and private rooms (**$$**), lockers with charging points, patio, bar, information, tours and classes can be arranged, good Palermo Soho location.

$ pp Casa Esmeralda, Honduras 5765, T4772 2446, www.casaesmeralda. com.ar. Laid-back, dorms and doubles (**$$**), neat garden with hammocks. Offers basic comfort with great charm.

$ pp Hostal El Candil, Lerma 476, T4899 1547, www.hostalelcandil.com. Argentine/Italian-owned hostel with shared rooms and doubles (**$$**), international atmosphere, quiet, comfortable, welcoming, rooftop terrace, tours arranged.

$ pp Hostel Suites Palermo, Charcas 4752, T4773 0806, www.suitespalermo. com. A beautiful century-old residence with the original grandeur partially preserved and a quiet atmosphere. Comfortable renovated dorms and private rooms with bath (**$$** doubles), good service, small travel agency, free internet, Wi-Fi, cooking and laundry facilities, DVD room and breakfast included. Free transfer from Ezeiza airport. HI discount.

San Telmo and around *p103, map p104*

$$$$ Mansión Dandi Royal, Piedras 922, T4361 3537, www.hotelmansion dandiroyal.com. A wonderfully restored 1903 residence, small upmarket hotel with an elegant tango atmosphere, small pool, good value. Daily tango lessons and *milonga* every Fri at 2130.

$$$$-$$$ Axel Hotel, Venezuela 649, T4136 9393, www.axelhotels.com. Stunning gay hotel with 5 floors of stylishly designed rooms, each floor with a cosy living area, rooftop pool, gourmet restaurant. Recommended.

$$$$-$$$ La Cayetana Historic House, México 1330, T4383 2230, www.lacayetanahotel.com.ar. 11 suites in a beautifully restored 1820s house, each room individually designed, quiet, buffet breakfast, parking. Recommended.

$$$ La Casita de San Telmo, Cochabamba 286, T4307 5073, www.lacasitadesantelmo.com. 7 rooms in restored 1840s house, most open onto a garden with a beautiful fig tree, owners are tango fans; rooms rented by day, week or month.

$$$ Lola House, Castro Barros 1073, Boedo, T4932 2139, www.lolahouse. com.ar. Small boutique hotel in a nicely refurbished house, welcoming owners, comfortable, safe; 10 mins from centre on Subte E, also on bus routes.

$$$ Lugar Gay de Buenos Aires, Defensa 1120 (no sign), T4300 4747, www.lugargay.com.ar. A men-only gay B&B with 8 comfortable rooms, video room, jacuzzi, a stone's throw from Plaza Dorrego.

$$$ Telmho, Defensa 1086, T4116 5467, www.telmho-hotel.com.ar. Smart rooms overlooking Plaza Dorrego, huge beds, modern bathrooms, lovely roof garden, helpful staff.

Youth hostels

$ pp Art Factory, Piedras 545, T4343 1463, www.artfactoryba.com.ar. Large, early 1900s house converted into a hostel, informal atmosphere with individually designed and brightly painted private rooms (some with bath, **$$**), dorms, halfway between the centre and San Telmo.

$ pp Circus, Chacabuco 1020, T4300 4983, www.hostelcircus.com. Stylish rooms for 2 (**$$**) to 4 people, tastefully renovated building, small heated swimming pool, bar and restaurant.

$ pp Garden House, Av San Juan 1271, T4304 1824, www.gardenhouse ba.com.ar. Small, welcoming independent hostel for those who don't want a party atmosphere; good barbecues on the terrace. Dorms and some doubles (**$$**). Recommended.

$ pp Hostal de Granados, Chile 374, T4362 5600, www.hostaldegranados. com.ar. Small, light, well-equipped rooms in an interesting building on a popular street, rooms for 2 (**$$**), dorms for 4 to 8, laundry.

$ pp Hostel-Inn Buenos Aires, Humberto Primo 820, T4300 7992, www.hibuenosaires.com. An old 2-storey mansion with dorms for up to 8 people and also private rooms (**$$**), activities, loud parties, individual lockers in every room. HI discount.

$ pp Kilca Hostel & Backpacker, México 1545, between Sáenz Peña and Virrey Cevallos, T4381 1966, www. kilcabackpacker.com. In a restored 19th-century house with attractive landscaped patios. A variety of rooms from dorms to doubles; all bathrooms shared, but 1 double with bath (**$$**).

$ pp Ostinatto, Chile 680, T4362 9639, www.ostinatto.com. Shared rooms, also has double rooms with and without bath (**$$**), and apartments for rent. Minimalist contemporary design in a 1920s building, very nice, promotes the arts, music, piano bar, movie room, tango lessons, arranges events, rooftop terrace.

$ pp Sabatico Travelers Hostel, México 1410, T4381 1138, www. sabaticohostel.com.ar. Dorms and double rooms with and without bath (**$$**), full range of services and information, rooftop barbecue, mini pool and bar. Good location.

Apartments/self-catering/ homestays

B&T Argentina, T4876 5000, www. bytargentina.com. Accommodation in student residences and host families; also furnished flats.

Bahouse, www.bahouse.com.ar. Very good flats, by the week or month, all furnished and well located in San Telmo, Retiro, Recoleta, Belgrano, Palermo and the centre.
Casa 34, Nicaragua 6045, T4775 0207, www.casa34.com. Helpful, with a big range.
Tu Casa Argentina, Fitzroy 2179, T4773 5544, www.tucasargentina.com. Furnished flats by the day, week, month (from US$55 per day). Credit cards not accepted, deposit and rent payable in dollars. Efficient and helpful.

Tigre *p105*
$$$$ La Becasina, Arroyo Las Cañas (Delta islands second section), T4328 2687, www.labecasina.com. One of Argentina's most delightful places to stay, an hour by launch from Tigre, buried deep from the outside world, with 15 individual lodges on stilts in the water, connected by wooden walkways, all comforts and luxuries provided and tasteful decor, with intimate dining room, jacuzzi and pool amidst the trees. Full board, excellent food and service. Recommended.
$$$$ Villa Julia, Paseo Victorica 800, in Tigre itself, T4749 0642, www. villajulia.com.ar. A 1906 villa converted into a chic hotel, beautifully restored fittings, comfortable, good restaurant open to non-residents.
$$$ Los Pecanes, on Arroyo Felicaria, T4728 1932, www.hosterialospecanes. com. On a secluded island visited regularly by hummingbirds. Ana and Richard offer a few comfortable rooms and delicious food. Ideal base for boat excursions and birdwatching. Cheaper Mon-Fri.
$$$-$ Posada de 1860, Av Libertador 190, T4749 4034, www.tigrehostel. com.ar. A beautiful stylish villa with suites and an associated **Hostel Tigre** at No 137 (same phone and website) with dorms for up to 6 (**$** pp), and private rooms (**$$$** double).
$$ TAMET, Río Carapachay Km 24, T4728 0055, www.tamet.com.ar. For a relaxing stay on an island with sandy beaches and quite comfortable premises, with breakfast, games and canoes. Also has camping.

⑦ Restaurants

Eating out in Buenos Aires is one of the city's great pleasures, with a huge variety of restaurants from the chic to the cheap. To try some of Argentina's excellent steak, choose from one of the many *parrillas*, where your huge slab of lean meat will be expertly cooked over a wood fire. If in doubt about where to eat, head for Puerto Madero, the revamped docks area, an attractive place to stroll along the waterfront before dinner. There are good places here, generally in stylish interiors, serving international as well as local cuisine, with good service if a little overpriced. Take a radio taxi to Palermo or Las Cañitas for a wide range of excellent restaurants all within strolling distance. For more information on the gastronomy of Buenos Aires see: www.guiaoleo. com.ar, restaurant guide in Spanish.
    There is a growing interest in less conventional eating out, from secret,

or *puerta cerrada*, restaurants, to local eateries off the normal restaurant circuit, exploring local markets and so on. 2 fantastic food-oriented blogs in English are: www.saltshaker.net, chef Dan Perlman who also runs a highly recommended private restaurant in his house, see website for details; and www.buenosairesfoodies.com. Another highly regarded closed-door option can be found at **The Argentine Experience**, http://theargentineexperience.com, while tours are run by **Parrilla Tour Buenos Aires**, http://parrillatour.com/.

Some restaurants are *tenedor libre*: eat as much as you like for a fixed price. Most cafés serve tea or coffee plus *facturas* (pastries) for breakfast.

Centre *p94, map p96*
$$$ Dadá, San Martín 941.
A restaurant and bar with eclectic decoration. Good for gourmet lunches.
$$$ Sorrento, Av Corrientes 668 (just off Florida). Intimate, elegant atmosphere, one of the most traditional places in the centre for very good pastas and seafood.
$$$ Tancat, Paraguay 645.
Delicious Spanish food, very popular at lunchtime.
$$$-$$ Gijón, Chile y San José. Very good-value *parrilla* at this popular *bodegón*, south of Congreso district.
$$ Al paso y algo más, San Martín 487. Open till 1630. Recommended choice for *choripan* and *churrasquito* sandwiches plus other meat dishes, cramped at lunchtime.
$$ Fikä, Hipólito Yrigoyen 782. Mon-Fri open till 1900, Sat closes

at 1600. Popular at lunchtime with a varied menu, is also attractive for a coffee break or a drink.
$$ Gianni´s, San Martín 430 and Reconquista 1028. The set menu with the meal-of-the-day makes an ideal lunch. Good risottos and salads. Slow service; open till 1700.
$$ Güerrín, Av Corrientes 1368.
A Buenos Aires institution. Serves filling pizza and *faina* (chick pea polenta) which you eat standing up at a bar, or at tables, though you miss out on the colourful local life that way. For an extra service fee, upstairs room is less crowded or noisy.
$$ Las Cuartetas, Av Corrientes 838.
A local institution open early to very late for fantastic pizza, can be busy and noisy as it's so popular.
$$ Sam Bucherie, 25 de Mayo 562.
Open till 1800. The most imaginative sandwiches and salads downtown.

Cafés
Café Tortoni, Av de Mayo 825-9. This most famous Buenos Aires café has been the elegant haunt of artists and writers for over 100 years, with marble columns, stained-glass ceilings, old leather chairs, and photographs of its famous clientele on the walls. Live tango. Packed with tourists, pricey, but still worth a visit.
Confitería Ideal, Suipacha 384.
One of the most atmospheric cafés in the city. Wonderfully old-fashioned 1930s interior, serving good coffee and excellent cakes with good service. See Tango shows, page 118.
El Gato Negro, Av Corrientes 1669.
A beautiful tearoom, serving a choice

of coffees and teas, and good cakes. Delightfully scented from the wide range of spices on sale.

Florida Garden, Florida y Paraguay. Another well-known café, popular for lunch, and tea.

Ice cream

The Italian ice cream tradition has been marked for decades by '*heladerías*' such as **Cadore**, Av Corrientes 1695, or **El Vesuvio**, Av Corrientes 1181, the oldest of all.

North of Plaza de Mayo *p98, map p100*

3 blocks west of Plaza San Martín, under the flyover at the northern end of Av 9 de Julio, between Arroyo and Av del Libertador in La Recova, are several recommended restaurants.
$$$ El Mirasol de la Recova, Posadas 1032. Serves top-quality *parrilla* in an elegant atmosphere.
$$$ Juana M, Carlos Pellegrini 1535 (downstairs). Excellent choice, popular with locals for its good range of dishes, and its very good salad bar.

Recoleta *p99, map p100*

$$$ Rodi Bar, Vicente López 1900. Excellent *bife* and other dishes in this typical *bodegón*, welcoming and unpretentious.
$$$ Sirop & Folie, Pasaje del Correo, Vte Lopez 1661, T4813 5900. Delightful chic design, delicious French-inspired food, superb patisserie too. Highly recommended.
$$$-$$ La Madeleine, Av Santa Fe 1726. Bright and cheerful choice, quite good pastas.

$$$-$$ María de Bambi, Ayacucho 1821 (with a small branch at Arenales 920). Open till 2130, closed on Sun. This small, quiet place is probably the best value in the area, serving very good and simple meals, also *salón de té* and patisserie.

Tea rooms, café/bars and ice cream

Arkakao, Av Quintana 188. Great ice creams at this elegant tea room.
Bröet, Azcuénaga 1144, www.broet. com.ar. Austrian-owned artisanal bakery with traditionally made bread from around the world.
Clásica y Moderna, Av Callao 892, T4812 8707, www.clasicaymoderna. com. One of the city's most welcoming cafés, with a bookshop, great atmosphere, good breakfast through to drinks at night, daily live music and varied shows.
Como en casa, Av Quintana 2, Riobamba 1239, Laprida 1782 and at San Martín y Viamonte (former convent of Santa Catalina). Very popular in the afternoon for its varied and delicious cakes and fruit pies.
Freddo, and **Un'Altra Volta**, ice cream parlours, both with several branches in the city.
Milion, Paraná 1048. Stylish bar and café in an elegant mansion with marble stairs and a garden, good drinks, mixed clientèle. Recommended Fri after midnight.

Palermo *p99, map p100*

This area of Buenos Aires is very popular, with many chic restaurants and bars in Palermo Viejo (referred to as 'Palermo Soho' for the area next to Plaza Cortázar and 'Palermo Hollywood' for the area beyond the railways and Av Juan B Justo) and the Las Cañitas district. It's a sprawling district, so you could take a taxi to one of these restaurants, and walk around before deciding where to eat. It's also a great place to stop for lunch, with cobbled streets, and 1900s buildings, now housing chic clothes shops. The Las Cañitas area is fashionable, with a wide range of interesting restaurants mostly along Báez, and most opening at around 2000, though only open for lunch at weekends:

$$$ Bio, Humboldt 2192, T4774 3880. Open daily. Delicious gourmet organic food, on a sunny corner.

$$$ Campobravo, Báez y Arévalo and Honduras y Fitz Roy. Stylish, minimalist, superb steaks and vegetables on the *parrilla*. Popular and recommended, can be noisy.

$$$ El Manto, Costa Rica 5801, T4774 2409. Genuine Armenian dishes, relaxed, good for a quiet evening.

$$$ El Preferido de Palermo, Borges y Guatemala, T4774 6585. Very popular *bodegón* serving both Argentine and Spanish-style dishes.

$$$ Janio, Malabia 1805, T4833 6540. Open for breakfast through to the early hours. One of Palermo's first restaurants, sophisticated Argentine cuisine in the evening.

$$$ La Cabrera, Cabrera 5127 and 5099. Superb *parrilla* and pasta, huge portions, with 2 branches; very popular. They offer a sparkling white wine while you wait.

$$$ Morelia, Baez 260 and Humboldt 2005. Cooks superb pizzas on the *parrilla*, and has a lovely roof terrace for summer.

$$$ Siamo nel forno, Costa Rica 5886. Excellent true Italian pizzas, recommended tiramisu.

$$$ Social Paraíso, Honduras 5182. Closed Sun evening and Mon. Simple delicious dishes in a relaxed chic atmosphere, with a lovely patio at the back. Good fish and tasty salads.

$$ Krishna, Malabia 1833. A small, intimate place serving Indian-flavoured vegetarian dishes.

Tea rooms, café/bars and ice cream

Palermo has good cafés opposite the park on Av del Libertador.

Cusic, El Salvador 6016, T4139 9173, www.cusic.com.ar. Closed Mon. For breakfast and lunches, breads, sandwiches, wraps, puddings.

Persicco, Honduras 4900, Salguero y Cabello, Av Santa Fe 3212, Maure y Migueletes, Tucumán y Reconquista (Centre) and Av Rivadavia 4933 (Caballito). The grandsons of **Freddo**'s founders also offer excellent ice cream.

San Telmo *p103, map p104*

$$$ Brasserie Petanque, Defensa y México. Very attractive, informal French restaurant offering a varied menu with very good, creative dishes. Excellent value for their set lunch menus.

$$$ Gran Parrilla del Plata, Chile 594, T4300 8858, www.parrilladelplata. com. Popular, good value *parrilla* on a historic corner.

\$\$\$ La Brigada, Estados Unidos 465, T4361 5557. Excellent *parrilla*, serving Argentine cuisine and wines. Very popular, expensive. Always reserve.
\$\$\$-\$\$ Naturaleza Sabia, Balcarce 958. Tasty vegetarian and vegan dishes in an attractive ambience.

Tea rooms, café/bars and ice cream

Británico, Brasil y Defensa 399. Open 24 hrs. A historic place with a good atmosphere at lunchtime.
Dorrego, Humberto Primo y Defensa. Bar/café with great atmosphere, seating on plaza outside, good for late-night coffee or drinks.
Dylan, Perú 1086. Very good ice cream.
La Poesía, Chile y Bolívar. Ideal for a coffee break on the sunny sidewalk.
Nonna Bianca, Estados Unidos 425. For ice cream in an internet café.
Pride Café, Balcarce y Giuffra. Wonderful sandwiches, juices, salads and brownies, with lots of magazines to read.

Puerto Madero (Docks) *p105*
map p93
\$\$\$ Cabaña Las Lilas, Av Moreau de Justo 516, T4313 1336. Reputedly one of the finest *parrillas* in town, pricey and popular with foreigners and business people.
\$\$\$ Le Grill, Av Moreau de Justo 876, T4331 0454. A gourmet touch at a sophisticated *parrilla* which includes dry-aged beef, pork and lamb on its menu.

🐾 Bars and clubs

Generally it is not worth going to clubs before 0230 at weekends. Dress is usually smart. Entry can be from US\$10-15, sometimes including a drink. A good way to visit some of the best bars is to join a pub crawl, eg **The Buenos Aires Pub Crawl**, www.buenosairespubcrawl.com, whose daily crawls are a safe night out.

Bars
Buller Brewing Company, Roberto M Ortiz 1827, Recoleta, www.bullerpub. com. Brew pub which also serves international food.
Casa Bar, Rodríguez Peña 1150, Recoleta. Beers from around the world in a restored mansion, good place to watch international sports matches, also serves food.
La Cigale, 25 de Mayo 597, Centre, T4893 2332. Popular after office hours, good live music.
Mundo Bizarro, Serrano 1222. Famous for its weird films, cocktails, American-style food, electronic and pop music.
Seddon, Defensa y Chile. Traditional bar open till late with live music on Fri.
Sugar, Costa Rica 4619. Welcoming bar with cheap beer and drinks, happy hour nightly, shows international sports.

The corner of Reconquista and Marcelo T de Alvear in Retiro is the centre of the small 'Irish' pub district, overcrowded on St Patrick's Day, 17 Mar. **Druid In**, Reconquista 1040, Centre, is by far the most attractive choice there, open for lunch and with live music weekly. **The Shamrock**,

Rodríguez Peña 1220, in Recoleta, is another Irish-run, popular bar, happy hour for ISIC holders.

Clubs
Bahrein, Lavalle 345, Centre, www. bahreinba.com. Funky and electronic.
L'Arc, Niceto Vega 5452, Palermo. Hosts The X Club weekly, with a cocktail bar and live bands.
Niceto Club, Niceto Vega 5510, Palermo, T4779 9396, www.nicetoclub. com. Early live shows and dancing afterwards. Club 69 weekly parties for house, electronic, hip hop and funk music.

Gay clubs Most gay clubs charge from US$10 entry. **Amerika**, Gascón 1040, Almagro, www.ameri-k.com.ar, Fri-Sun, attracting more than 2000 party-goers over 3 floors; **Bach Bar**, Cabrera 4390, www.bach-bar.com.ar, a friendly lesbian bar in Palermo Viejo, Wed-Sun; **Sitges**, Av Córdoba 4119, Palermo, T4861 3763, www.sitges online.com.ar, a gay and lesbian bar.

Jazz clubs Notorious, Av Callao 966, T4813 6888, www.notorious. com.ar. Live jazz at a music shop with bar and restaurant. **Thelonious**, Salguero 1884, www.thelonious.com. ar, T4829 1562, for live jazz and DJs; **Virasoro Bar**, Guatemala 4328, www. virasorobar.com.ar, T4831 8918, for live jazz in a 1920s art deco house.

Salsa clubs La Salsera, Yatay 961, T4866 1829, www.lasalsera.com, is highly regarded.

☻ Entertainment

At carnival time, look for the **Programa Carnaval Porteño** (it's on Facebook).

Cinemas
The selection of films is excellent, ranging from new Hollywood releases to Argentine and world cinema; details are listed daily in main newspapers. Films are shown uncensored and most foreign films are subtitled. Tickets best booked early afternoon to ensure good seats (average price US$9, discount on Wed and for 1st show daily).

Independent foreign and national films are shown during the **Festival de Cine Independiente** (BAFICI), www.bafici.gov.ar, held every Apr.

Cultural events
Centro Cultural Borges, Galerías Pacífico, Viamonte y San Martín, p 1, T5555 5359, www.ccborges.org.ar. Art exhibitions, concerts, film shows and ballet; some student discounts.
Ciudad Cultural Konex, Sarmiento 3131 (Abasto), T4864 3200, www. ciudadculturalkonex.org. A converted oil factory hosts this huge complex holding plays, live music shows, summer film projections under the stars, modern ballet, puppet theatre and, occasionally, massive parties.
Usina del Arte, Caffarena y Av Pedro de Mendoza (La Boca), www.usina delarte.org. Temporary art exhibitions, plays, live music, film shows at an impressive 1910s converted power station which also offers guided visits.
Villa Ocampo, Elortondo 1811, Beccar, Partido de San Isidro, T4732 4988, www.

villaocampo.org. Former residence of writer and founder of Revista Sur Victoria Ocampo, now owned by UNESCO, in northern suburbs, Thu-Sun and holidays 1230-1800, US$2.50 (weekends and holidays US$4) entry, open for visits, courses, exhibitions and meals at its café/restaurant.

See also the programmes of the **Alliance Française**, www.alianzafrancesa.org.ar, **British Arts Centre**, www.britishartscentre.org.ar, **Goethe Institut**, www.goethe.de/ins/ar/bue/esindex.htm, and **Instituto Cultural Argentino Norteamericano**, www.icana.org.ar.

Tango shows

There are 2 ways to enjoy tango: you can watch the dancing at a tango show. Most pride themselves on very high standards and, although they are not cheap (show only US$50-90, show and dinner US$75-150), this is tango at its best. Most prices include drinks and hotel transfers. Or you can learn to dance at a class and try your steps at a *milonga* (tango club). The Tango page on www.turismo.buenosaires.gob.ar lists *tanguerías* for tango shows, classes and *milongas*.

See also the websites **www.tangocity.com** and **www.todotango.com**.

Every Aug there is a tango dancing competition, **Festival y Mundial de Baile**, open to both locals and foreigners.

Bar Sur, Estados Unidos 299, T4362 6086, www.bar-sur.com.ar. Open 2000-0200. Price with or without dinner. Good fun, public sometimes join the professional dancers.

El Querandí, Perú 302, T5199 1770, www.querandi.com.ar. Daily shows, with or without dinner, also open for lunch. Tango show restaurant, dating back to 1920s.

El Viejo Almacén, Independencia y Balcarce, T4307 7388, www.viejoalmacen.com.ar. Daily, dinner from 2000, show 2200. Impressive dancing and singing. Recommended.

Esquina Carlos Gardel, Carlos Gardel 3200 y Anchorena, T4867 6363, www.esquinacarlosgardel.com.ar. Opposite the former Mercado del Abasto, this is the most popular venue in Gardel's own neighbourhood; dinner at 2030, show at 2230. Recommended.

Esquina Homero Manzi, Av San Juan 3601 (Subte Boedo), T4957 8488, www.esquinahomeromanzi.com.ar. Traditional show at 2200 with excellent musicians and dancers, dinner (2100) and show available, tango school. Recommended.

Piazzolla Tango, Florida 165 (basement), Galería Güemes, T4344 8201, www.piazzollatango.com. A beautifully restored belle époque hall hosts a smart tango show; dinner at 2045, show at 2215.

Milongas These are very popular with younger *porteños*. You can take a class and get a feel for the music before the dancing starts a couple of hours later. Both tango and *milonga* (the music that contributed to the origins of tango and is more cheerful) are played. Cost is from US$8; even beginners are welcome.

Centro Cultural Torquato Tasso, Defensa 1575, T4307 6506, www.

torquatotasso.com.ar. See web for programme and prices (daily lessons), English spoken.

Confitería Ideal, Suipacha 384, T4328 7750, www.confiteriaideal.com. Very atmospheric ballroom for daily *milongas* at this old central café. Most days dancing starts as early as 1500; lessons start 1230 on some days, 1530 on others (not on Sun). Also evening tango shows.

La Viruta (at Centro Armenio), Armenia 1366, Palermo Viejo, T4774 6357, www.lavirutatango.com. Very popular, classes every day except Mon, entry US$7 (check website for times), also salsa and rock dancing classes, with restaurant.

Theatre

About 20 commercial theatres play all year and there are many amateur theatres. The main theatre street is Av Corrientes.

Complejo Teatral de Buenos Aires, Corrientes 1530, T4371 0111/8, http://complejoteatral.gob.ar, is a group of 5 theatres with many cultural activities. Book seats for theatre, ballet and opera as early as possible. Tickets for most popular shows (including rock and pop concerts) are sold also through **Ticketek**, T5237 7200, www.ticketek.com.ar. See also www.alternativateatral.com and www.mundoteatral.com.ar. For live Argentine and Latin American bands, best venues are: **La Trastienda**, Balcarce 460, San Telmo, www.latrastienda.com, theatre/café with lots of live events, also serving meals and drinks from breakfast to dinner, great music; or **ND Teatro**, Paraguay 918, www.ndteatro.com.ar.

○ Shopping

The main, fashionable shopping streets are Florida and Santa Fe (from Av 9 de Julio to Av Pueyrredón). Palermo is the best area for chic boutiques and well-known international fashion labels; head for C Honduras and C El Salvador, between Malabia and Serrano. C Defensa in San Telmo is known for its antique shops. It also has a few craft stalls around C Alsina, Fri 1000-1700. **Pasaje de la Defensa**, Defensa 1179, is a beautifully restored 1880s house containing small shops.

Bookshops

Buenos Aires is renowned for its bookshops and was UNESCO's World Book Capital in 2011. Many shops are along Florida, Av Corrientes (from Av 9 de Julio to Callao) or Av Santa Fe, and in shopping malls. Second-hand and discount bookshops are mostly along Av Corrientes and Av de Mayo. Rare books are sold in several specialized stores in the Microcentro (the area enclosed by Suipacha, Esmeralda, Tucumán and Paraguay). The main chains of bookshops, usually selling a small selection of foreign books are: **Cúspide**, **Distal**, **Kel** (imported books, mostly in English) and **Yenny-El Ateneo**, whose biggest store is on Av Santa Fe 1860, in an old theatre; there is café where the stage used to be. **Eterna Cadencia**, Honduras 5574, T4774 4100, www.eternacadencia. com. Has an excellent selection and a good café. **Walrus Books**, Estados Unidos 617, San Telmo, T4300 7135, www.walrus-books.com.ar. Sells second-hand books in English, including Latin American authors, good children's section.

Handicrafts
Arte y Esperanza, Balcarce 234 and Suipacha 892, www.artey esperanza.com.ar. Crafts made by indigenous communities, sold by a Fair Trade organization.
Artesanías Argentinas, Montevideo 1386, www.artesaniasargentinas. org. Aboriginal crafts and other traditional items sold by a Fair Trade organization.
El Boyero, Florida 753 (Galerías Pacífico) and 953, T4312 3564, http://es.elboyero.com. High-quality silver, leather, woodwork and other typical Argentine handicrafts.
Martín Fierro, Santa Fe 992. Good handicrafts, stonework, etc. Recommended.
Plata Nativa, Galería del Sol, Florida 860, local 41, www.platanativa.com. For Latin American folk handicrafts and high-quality jewellery.

In Dec there is a **Feria Internacional de Artesanías**.

Leather goods
Several shops are concentrated along Florida next to Plaza San Martín and also in Suipacha (900 block).
Aida, Galería de la Flor, local 30, Florida 670. Quality, inexpensive leather products, can make a leather jacket to measure in the same day.
Casa López, MT de Alvear 640/658, www.casalopez.com.ar. The most traditional and finest leather shop, expensive but worth it.

Dalla Fontana, Reconquista 735, www.dalla-fontana.com.ar. Leather factory, fast, efficient and reasonably priced for made-to-measure clothes.
Galería del Caminante, Florida 844. Has a variety of good shops with leather goods, arts and crafts, souvenirs, etc.
Prüne, Florida 963 and in many shopping centres, www.prune. com.ar. Fashionable designs for women, many options in leather and not very expensive.

Markets and malls
Markets can be found in many of the city's parks and plazas, which hold weekend fairs. You will find they all sell pretty much the same sort of handicrafts. The following offer something different:
Feria de Mataderos, Lisandro de la Torre y Av de los Corrales, T4342 9629, www.feriademataderos.com.ar, subte E to end of line then taxi (US$7), or buses 55, 63, 80, 92, 103, 117, 126, 141, 155, 180. Sat from 1700 (Jan-Feb), Sun 1100-2000 (Mar-Dec). Long way but few tourists, fair of Argentine handicrafts and traditions, music and dance festivals, gaucho horsemanship skills; nearby **Museo Criollo de los Corrales**, Av de los Corrales 6436, T4687 1949, Sun 1200-1830, US$0.20.
Mercado de las Luces, Manzana de las Luces, Perú y Alsina. Mon-Fri 1030-1930, Sun 1400-1930. Handicrafts, second-hand books, plastic arts.
Parque Centenario, Av Díaz Vélez y L Marechal. Sat-Sun and holidays 1100-2000, local crafts, cheap handmade clothes, used items of all sorts.

Parque Rivadavia, Av Rivadavia 4900. Sun 0900-1300. Second-hand books, stamps, coins, records, tapes, CDs and magazines.

Plaza Dorrego, San Telmo. Sun 1000-1700. For souvenirs, antiques, etc, with free tango performances and live music, wonderfully atmospheric, and an array of 'antiques'.

Plaza Italia, Santa Fe y Uriarte (Palermo). Sat 1200-2000, Sun 1000-2000. Second-hand textbooks and magazines (daily), handicrafts market.

The city has many fine shopping malls, including **Abasto de Buenos Aires**, Av Corrientes 3247, T4959 3400, nearest Subte: Carlos Gardel, line B, in the city's impressive, art deco former fruit and vegetable market building, and **Patio Bullrich**, Av del Libertador 750 and Posadas 1245, T4814 7400, nearest Subte: 8 blocks from Plaza San Martín, line C, the most upmarket mall in the city.

⊙ What to do

Cricket

Asociación Argentina de Cricket, Juan María Gutiérrez 3829, T3974 9593, www.cricketargentina.com, for information. Cricket is played Sep-Apr.

Cycle hire and tours

La Bicicleta Naranja, Pasaje Giuffra 308, San Telmo and Nicaragua 4825, Palermo, T4362 1104, www.labicicleta naranja.com.ar. Bike hire and tours to all parts of the city, 3-4 hrs.

Lan&Kramer Bike Tours, San Martín 910 p 6, T4311 5199, www.biketours. com.ar. Daily at 0930 and 1400 next to the monument of San Martín (Plaza

San Martín), 3½- to 4-hr cycle tours to the south or the north of the city; also to San Isidro and Tigre, 4½-5 hrs and full day tours, plus summer evening tours downtown; also, bike rental.

Urban biking, Maipú 971, T4314 2325, www.urbanbiking.com. 4½-hr tours either to the south or to the north of the centre, starting daily 0900 and 1400 from Av Santa Fe y Maipú; night city tours, 3½-4 hrs, full day tours to San Isidro and Tigre (including kayak in the Delta), or occasionally, to the pampas. Also rents bikes.

Football and rugby

Football fans should see **Boca Juniors**, matches every other Sun at their stadium (La Bombonera, Brandsen 805, La Boca, www.bocajuniors.com.ar, tickets for non-members only through tour operators, or the museum – see the murals), or their arch-rivals, **River Plate**, Av Figueroa Alcorta 7597, T4789 1200, www.cariverplate.com.ar. Football season Feb-Jun, and Aug-Dec, most matches on Sun. Buy tickets from stadiums, sports stores near the grounds, ticket agencies or hostels and hotels, which may arrange guide/ transport (don't take a bus if travelling alone, phone a radio taxi; see also **Tangol**, page 123). Rugby season Apr-Oct/ Nov. For more information, **Unión de Rugby de Buenos Aires**, www.urba. org.ar, or **Unión Argentina de Rugby**, T4898 8500, www.uar.com.ar.

Polo

The high handicap season is Sep-Dec, but it is played all year round. Argentina has the top polo players in the world. A visit to the national finals at Palermo in Nov and Dec is recommended. For information, **Asociación Argentina de Polo**, T4777 8005, www.aapolo.com.

Tour operators and travel agents
An excellent way of seeing Buenos Aires is on a 3-hr tour. Longer tours may include dinner and a tango show, or a boat trip in the Delta, or a gaucho fiesta at a ranch (great food and dancing). Bookable through most travel agents. See also **BA Free Tour**, www.bafree tour.com, www.buenosaireslocal tours.com and **City Walkers**, www.city walkers.com.ar, for free walking tours. For another type of walking tour, see **BA Street Art**, http://buenosairesstreet art.com, and **Graffitimundo**, http:// graffitimundo.com, who offer tours of the city's best graffiti, see websites for prices and times.
Anda, T3221 0833, www.andatravel. com.ar. Operator specializing in socially and environmentally responsible tourism in Buenos Aires and around the country, including volunteering opportunities.
Argentina Excepción, Costa Rica 5546, T4772 6620, www.argentina-excepcion.com. French/Argentine agency offering tailor-made, upper-end tours, fly-drives, themed trips and other services. Also has a Santiago branch, www.chile-excepcion.com.
BAT, Buenos Aires Tur, Lavalle 1444 of 10, T4371 2304, www.buenos airestur.com. City tours, twice daily; Tigre and Delta, daily, 5 hrs.
Buenos Aires Bus (**Bus Turístico**), www.buenosairesbus.com. Open

yellow double-decker buses follow 2 routes every 10-20 mins covering main sights from La Boca to Núñez with multilingual recorded tours. 1-day (US$27) and 2-day (US$33) hop-on/ hop-off tickets can be purchased online or onboard. Find bus stops on website or on map provided at city's tourist offices.
Buenos Aires Vision, Esmeralda 356, p 8, T4394 4682, www.buenosaires-vision.com.ar. City tours, Tigre and Delta, Tango (cheaper without dinner) and Fiesta Gaucha.
Cultour, T156-365 6892 (mob), www. cultour.com.ar. A highly recommended walking tour of the city, 3-4 hrs led by a group of Argentine history/tourism graduates. In English and Spanish.
Eternautas, Av Julio A Roca 584 p 7, T5031 9916, www.eternautas.com. Historical, cultural and artistic tours of the city and Pampas guided in English, French or Spanish by academics from the University of Buenos Aires, flexible.
Flyer Lufthansa City Center, Av Fondo De La Legua 425, San Isidro, T4512 8100, www.lcc-flyer.com. English, Dutch, German spoken, repeatedly recommended, especially for estancias, fishing, polo, motorhome rental.
Kallpa, Tucumán 861, p 2, T5278 8010, www.kallpatour.com. Tailor-made tours to natural and cultural destinations throughout the country, with an emphasis on adventure, conservation and golf.
Mai10, Av Córdoba 657, p 3, T4314 3390, www.mai10.com.ar. High-end, personalized tours for groups and individuals, covers the whole country, special interests include art, cuisine,

estancias, photo safaris, fishing and many more.

Say Hueque, Viamonte 749, p 6 of 1, and other branches in Palermo and San Telmo, T5258 8740, www.sayhueque.com. Recommended travel agency offering good-value tours aimed at independent travellers, friendly English-speaking staff.

Tangol, Florida 971, ground floor, shop 31, and Defensa 831, T4363 6000, www.tangol.com. Friendly, independent agency specializing in football and tango, plus various sports, such as polo and paragliding. Can arrange tours, plane and bus tickets, accommodation. English spoken. Discounts for students. Overland tours in Patagonia Oct-Apr.

⊖ Transport

Air

Ezeiza (officially Ministro Pistarini, T5480 6111, www.aa2000.com.ar), the international airport, is 35 km southwest of the centre (also handles some domestic flights). The airport has 3 terminals: 'A', 'B' and 'C'. There are duty free shops (expensive), ATM and exchange facilities at **Banco Nación** (terminal 'A') (only change the very minimum to get you into the city), a **Ministerio de Turismo** desk, and a post office (Mon-Fri 0900-1700, Sat 0900-1200). No hotels nearby, but there is an attractive B&B 5 mins away with transfer included: **$$$ Bernie's**, Estrada 186, Barrio Uno, T4480 0420, www.posadabernies.com, book in advance.

There is a **Devolución IVA/Tax Free** desk (return of VAT) for purchases over the value of AR$70 (ask for a Global Refund check plus the invoice from the shop when you buy). Hotel booking service at Tourist Information desk – helpful, but prices are higher if booked in this way.

Airport buses A display in immigration shows choices and prices of transport into the city. A good dual carriageway links with the General Paz highway which circles the city. The safest way between airport and city is by an airport bus service run every 30 mins by **Manuel Tienda León** (office in front of you as you arrive), company office and terminal at Av Madero 1299 y San Martín, behind Sheraton Hotel in Retiro (take a taxi from the terminal; do not walk outside), T4315 5115, www.tiendaleon.com.ar. The bus costs US$14 one way, pay by pesos, dollars, euros or credit card. **Manuel Tienda León** will also collect passengers from addresses in centre for a small extra fee, book the previous day. Bus from Ezeiza to Aeroparque, 1½ hrs, US$14. Remise taxis for up to 4 passengers (**Manuel Tienda León**, **Taxi Ezeiza**, www.taxiezeiza.com.ar, and other counters at Ezeiza) charge US$50 airport to town, but less from city to airport. Radio taxis charge US$45 (make sure you pay for your taxi at the booth and then wait in the queue), see Taxi, page 126, for more details. On no account take an unmarked car at Ezeiza, no matter how attractive the fare may sound. Drivers are adept at separating you from far more money than you can possibly owe them.

Always ask to see the taxi driver's licence. If you take an ordinary taxi the Policía de Seguridad Aeroportuaria on duty notes down the car's licence and time of departure.

Aeroparque (Jorge Newbery Airport), 4 km north of the centre, T5480 6111, www.aa2000.com.ar, handles all internal flights, and some flights to neighbouring countries. On the 1st floor there is a *patio de comidas* (food hall) and many shops. At the airport there is also tourist information, car rental, bus companies, ATM, public phones and luggage deposit (ask at information desk in sector B). **Manuel Tienda León** buses to Aeroparque (see above for address), more or less hourly; from Aeroparque, 0900-2330, 30-min journey, US$5. Local bus 45 run from outside the airport to the Retiro railway station. No 37 goes to **Palermo** and **Recoleta** and No 160 to **Palermo** and **Almagro**. If going to the airport, make sure it goes to Aeroparque by asking the driver. *Remise* taxis to **Ezeiza**, operated by **Manuel Tienda León**, US$50; to the city centre US$16. Taxi to centre US$8. **Manuel Tienda León** operates buses between Ezeiza and Aeroparque airports, US$14.

Bus

Local City buses are called *colectivos* and cover a very wide radius. They are clean, frequent, efficient and very fast. Colectivo fares are calculated in 3-km sections, US$0.50-0.60, but fares are cheaper if you have a pre-paid smart card called *Sube* (see www.xcolectivo.com.ar for details). If not using a smart card, have coins ready for ticket machine as drivers do not sell tickets, but may give change. The bus number is not always sufficient indication of destination, as each number may have a variety of routes, but bus stops display routes of buses stopping there and little plaques are displayed in the driver's window. A rapid transit system, **Metrobús**, incorporating existing bus routes, is being implemented, including along Av 9 de Julio. See www.omnilineas.com.ar for city guides listing bus routes.

Long distance Bus terminal for all international and interprovincial buses is at Ramos Mejía y Antártida Argentina (Subte Line C), behind Retiro station, T4310 0700, www.tebasa.com.ar. The terminal is on 3 floors.

Bus information is at the Ramos Mejía entrance on the middle floor. Ticket offices are on the upper floor, but there are hundreds of them so you'll need to consult the list of companies and their office numbers at the top of the escalator. They are organized by region and are colour coded. Buenos Aires city information desk is on the upper floor. It is advisable to go to the bus station the day before you travel to get to know where the platforms are so that when you are fully laden you know exactly where to go. At the basement and ground levels there are left-luggage lockers; tokens are sold in kiosks; for large baggage, there's a *guarda equipaje* on the lower floor. For further details of bus services and fares, look under proposed destinations. There are no direct buses to either of the airports.

International buses International services are run by both local and foreign companies; heavily booked Dec-Mar (especially at weekends), when most fares rise sharply. To **Uruguay**: Do not buy Uruguayan bus tickets in Buenos Aires; wait till you get to Colonia or Montevideo.
To **Montevideo**, **Bus de la Carrera**, **Cauvi** and **Cóndor Estrella**, US$51-59, 8 hrs; see Ferries, below.

Car
Driving in Buenos Aires is no problem, provided you have eyes in the back of your head and good nerves. Traffic fines are high and police look out for drivers without the correct papers. Car hire is cheaper if you arrange it when you arrive rather than from home.
Sixt, Cerrito 1314, www.sixt.com.ar, and national rental agencies, such as **Dietrich**, Cerrito 1575, T0800-999 2999, www.localizadietrich.com. **Ruta Sur**, Av General Paz 1260, T5238 4071, www.rutasur.eu. Rents 4WDs and motorhomes.

Ferry
To **Montevideo** and **Colonia** from Terminal Dársena Norte, Av Antártida Argentina 821 (2 blocks from Av Córdoba y Alem). **Buquebus**, T4316 6500, www.buquebus.com (tickets from Terminal, Retiro bus station, from offices at Av Córdoba 867 and Posadas 1452, by phone or online): **1)** Direct to **Montevideo**, 1-4 a day, 3 hrs, from US$105 tourist class, one way, also carries vehicles and motorcycles. **2)** To **Colonia**, services by 3 companies: **Buquebus**: minimum 5 crossings a

day, from 1-3 hrs, US$53 tourist class one way on slower vessel, US$72 tourist class on faster vessel, with bus connection to **Montevideo**. . (**Buquebus** also offers flights to Uruguay and Brazil with onward connections, www.flybqb.com.uy.)
Colonia Express, www.coloniaexpress. com, makes 2-3 crossings a day between Buenos Aires and Colonia in a fast catamaran (no vehicles carried), 50 mins, prices range from US$18 to US$35 one way, depending on type of service and where bought. Office is at Av Córdoba 753, T4317 4100; Terminal Fluvial is at Av Pedro de Mendoza 330. You must go there by taxi, US$8 from Retiro. **Seacat**, www. seacatcolonia.com, 3 fast ferries to Colonia, 1 hr, US$42 one way, from the same terminal as Buquebus, with bus to Montevideo (US$40-52) and Punta del Este (US$58-66) on most crossings. Office: Av Córdoba 772, T4322 9555, phone sales: T4314 5100.

Metro (Subte)
7 lines link the outer parts of the city to the centre. Line 'A' runs under Av Rivadavia, from Plaza de Mayo to San Pedrito (Flores). **Line 'B'** from central Post Office, on Av L N Alem, under Av Corrientes to Federico Lacroze railway station at Chacarita, ending at Juan Manuel de Rosas (Villa Urquiza). **Line 'C'** links Plaza Constitución with the Retiro railway station, and provides connections with all the other lines but 'H'.
Line 'D' runs from Plaza de Mayo (Catedral), under Av Roque Sáenz Peña (Diagonal Norte), Córdoba,

Santa Fe and Palermo to Congreso de Tucumán (Belgrano). Line 'E' runs from Plaza de Mayo (Cabildo, on C Bolívar) through San Juan to Plaza de los Virreyes (connection to Line 'P' or Premetro train service to the southwest end of the city). Line 'H' runs from Corrientes, via Once to Hospitales (Parque Patricios), under Av Jujuy and Av Almafuerte. Note that 3 stations, 9 de Julio (Line 'D'), Diagonal Norte (Line 'C') and Carlos Pellegrini (Line 'B') are linked by pedestrian tunnels. The fare is US$0.45, the same for any direct trip or combination between lines; magnetic cards (for 1, 2, 5, 10, or 30 journeys) must be bought at the station before boarding; only pesos accepted. Trains are operated by **Metrovías**, T0800-555 1616, www.metrovias.com.ar, and run Mon-Sat 0500-2220 (Sun 0800-2200). Line A, the oldest was built in 1913, the earliest in South America. Backpacks and luggage allowed. Free map (if available) from stations and tourist office.

Taxi

Taxis are painted yellow and black, and carry Taxi flags. Fares are shown in pesos. The meter starts at US$1.50 when the flag goes down; make sure it isn't running when you get in. A fixed rate of US$0.15 for every 200 m or 1-min wait is charged thereafter. The fare from 2200 to 0600 starts at US$1.80, plus US$0.18 for every 200 m or 1-min wait. A charge is sometimes made for each piece of hand baggage (ask first). About 10% tip expected. For security, take a *remise* or radio taxi

booked by phone or at the company's office. Check that the driver's licence is displayed. Lock doors on the inside. The 2 airports and Retiro bus station are notorious for unlicensed taxi crime; use the airport buses and *remises* listed on pages 123-124, and taxis from the official rank in the bus terminal which are registered with police and safe.

Radio taxis are managed by several different companies; extra fee US$0.90. Phone a radio taxi from your hotel (they can make recommendations), a phone box or *locutorio*, giving the address where you are, and you'll usually be collected within 10 mins. **City**, T4585 5544; **Porteño**, T4566 5777; **Premium**, T5238 0000; **Tiempo**, T4854 3838.

Remise taxis operate all over the city, run from an office and have no meter. The companies are identified by signs on the pavement. Fares are fixed and can be cheaper than regular taxis, verifiable by phoning the office, and items left in the car can easily be reclaimed. **Universal**, T4105 5555.

Train

There are 4 main terminals: **1) Retiro** (3 lines: **Mitre**, **Belgrano** and **San Martín** in separate buildings). The state of services changes all the time, owing largely to poor maintenance. The independent website, www. sateliteferroviario.com.ar, is a good source of information on all services. Urban and suburban services include: Mitre line (T0800-222 8736) to **Belgrano**, **Mitre** (connection to Tren de la Costa, see page 128), **Olivos**, **San Isidro**, and **Tigre** (see page 105); long-distance services to **Rosario Norte**, 7½ hrs, US$3-7; to **Tucumán** via Rosario, Mon and Fri, 0728 (return Wed 1552, Sat 1900), an extra weekly service is added in summer, 26½ hrs, US$50 sleeper (for 2, breakfast included), US$17 pullman, US$9 1st class, US$5 *turista* (run by **Ferrocentral**, T0800-1221 8736, www.ferrocentralsa.com.ar). To **Córdoba** via Rosario, Mon and Thu 2035 (return Wed and Sun 1439), 17 hrs, US$38 sleeper (for 2, breakfast included), US$11.50 pullman, US$6.50 1st class, US$4 *turista* (run by **Ferrocentral**). Belgrano line to northwestern suburbs, including Villa Rosa, run by **Ferrovías**, T0800-777 3377. San Martín line for services to Pilar and long-distance services to Junín and Alberdi (see www.ferrobaires.gba.gov.ar).

2) Constitución, Roca line urban and suburban services to La Plata, Ezeiza, Ranelagh and Quilmes. Long-distance services (run by **Ferrobaires**, T4304 0028, www.ferrobaires.gba.gov.ar): **Bahía Blanca**, 5 a week 1945, 14 hrs, US$15-22. Also services to **Mar del Plata** (3 a week in early 2014, US$21-26) and Tandil.

3) Federico Lacroze, Urquiza line and Metro headquarters (run by **Metrovías**, T0800-555 1616, www.metrovias.com.ar). Suburban services: to General Lemos.

4) Once, Sarmiento line, urban and suburban services to Moreno and Luján. Long-distance services to Lincoln (run by **Ferrobaires**).

Tram

Old-fashioned street cars operate Mar-Nov on Sat and holidays 1600-1930 and Sun 1000-1300, 1600-1930 and Dec-Feb on Sat and holidays 1700-2030, Sun 1000-1300, 1700-2030, free, on a circular route along the streets of Caballito district, from C Emilio Mitre 500, Subte Primera Junta (Line A) or Emilio Mitre (Line E), no stops en route. Operated by **Asociación Amigos del Tranvía**, T4431 1073, www.tranvia.org.ar.

Tigre *p105*
Bus

From central **Buenos Aires**: take No 60 from Constitución: the 60 'bajo' is a little longer than the 60 'alto' but is better for sightseeing.

Ferry

To **Carmelo** (Uruguay) from Terminal Internacional, Lavalle 520, Tigre. **Cacciola**, T4749 0931, www.cacciolaviajes.com (in Buenos Aires at Florida 520, p 1, of 113, T4393 6100), 2 a day, 2½ hrs, US$42. To Montevideo (bus from Carmelo), 5½ hrs, US$52. To **Nueva Palmira** (Uruguay) from Terminal Internacional. **Líneas Delta Argentino**, oficina 6 at Estación Fluvial, T4731 1236, www.lineasdelta.com.ar. Daily at 0730, 3 hrs, US$30, US$47 return. To **Carmelo** US$35, US$53 return, and **Colonia**, 4½ hrs from Tigre, US$45, US$63 return, both daily 0730. **Note** Argentine port taxes are generally included in the fares for Argentine departures.

Train

From **Buenos Aires**: Mitre line from Retiro. Alternatively **Tren de la Costa**, T3220 6300, US$3.35 one way from Maipú station (reached by Mitre line from Retiro) to Delta station (Tigre) every 30 mins. (Buses to Tren de la Costa are No 60 from Constitución, No 19 or 71 from Once, No 152 from centre.) Terminus, Estación Delta, has the huge funfair, El Parque de la Costa, and a casino.

❶ Directory

Banks

ATMs are widespread for MasterCard or Visa. The financial district lies within a small area north of Plaza de Mayo, between Rivadavia, 25 de Mayo, Av Corrientes and Florida. In non-central areas find banks/ ATMs along the main avenues. Banks open Mon-Fri 1000-1500. Casas de cambio include **Banco Piano**, San Martín 345, T4321 9200, www.banco piano.com.ar, changes all TCs (commission 2%). **Forex**, MT de Alvear 540, T4010 2000. Other South American currencies can only be exchanged in *casas de cambio*.

Embassies and consulates

For all foreign embassies and consulates in Buenos Aires, see http://embassy.goabroad.com.

Language schools

Academia Buenos Aires, Hipólito Yrigoyen 571, p 4, T4345 5954, www.academiabuenosaires.com. **All-Spanish**, Talcahuano 77 p 1, T4832 7794, www.all-spanish.com.ar. One-to-one classes. **Amauta Spanish School**, Federico Lacroze 2129, T4777 2130, www.amautaspanish.com. Spanish classes, one-to-one or small groups, centres in Buenos Aires, Bariloche and at an estancia in the pampas. **Argentina I.L.E.E**, T4782 7173, www.argentinailee.com. Recommended by individuals and organizations alike, with a school in Bariloche. **Cedic**, Reconquista 715, p 11 E, T4312 1016, www.cedic.com.ar. Recommended. **Elebaires**, Av de Mayo 1370, of 10, p 3, T4383 7706, www.elebaires.com.ar. Small school with focused classes, also offers one-to-one lessons and excursions. Recommended. **Expanish**, Perón 698, T5252 3040, www.expanish.com. Well-organized courses which can involve excursions, accommodation and Spanish lessons in sister schools in Peru and Chile. Highly recommended. **IBL (Argentina Spanish School)**, Florida 165, p 3, of 328, T4331 4250, www.ibl.com.ar. Group and one-to-one lessons, all levels, recommended. **Bue Spanish School**, Av Belgrano 1431, p 2, apt18, T4381 6347, www.buespanish.com.ar. Intensive and regular Spanish courses, culture programme, free materials. **Laboratorio de Idiomas (Universidad de Buenos Aires)**, 25 de Mayo 221 (also other branches), T4334 7512 or T4343 1196, www.idiomas. filo.uba.ar. Offers cheap, coherent courses, including summer intensive courses. For other schools teaching Spanish, and for private tutors look in *Buenos Aires Herald* in the classified advertisements. Enquire also at **Asatej** (see Useful addresses, below).

Medical services

Urgent medical service: for free municipal ambulance service to an emergency hospital department (day and night) **Casualty ward**, **Sala de guardia**, T107 or T4923 1051/58 (SAME). Inoculations: **Hospital Rivadavia**, Av Las Heras 2670, T4809 2000, Mon-Fri 0700-1200 (bus Nos 10, 37, 59, 60, 62, 92, 93 or 102 from Plaza Constitución), or **Dirección de Sanidad de Fronteras y Terminales de Transporte**, Ing Huergo 690, T4343 1190, Mon-Fri 1000-1500, bus No 20 from Retiro, no appointment required (yellow fever only; take passport). If not provided, buy the vaccines in **Laboratorio Biol**, Uriburu 153, T4953 7215, or in larger chemists. Many chemists have signs indicating that they give injections. Any hospital with an infectology department will give hepatitis A. **Centros Médicos Stamboulian**, 25 de Mayo 464, T4515 3000, Pacheco de Melo 2941, also in Belgrano, Villa Crespo, Villa Urquiza and Flores, www.stamboulian.com.ar. Private health advice for travellers and inoculations centre. Public Hospitals: **Hospital Argerich**, Almte Brown esq Py y Margall 750, T4121 0700. **Hospital Juan A Fernández**, Cerviño y Bulnes, T4808 2600/2650, probably the best free medical attention in the city. **British Hospital**, Perdriel 74, T4309 6400, www.hospital britanico.org.ar. **German Hospital**, Av Pueyrredón 1640, between Beruti and Juncal, T4827 7000, www.hospitalaleman. com.ar. Both have first-aid centres (*centros asistenciales*) as do other main hospitals. Dental treatment: excellent dental treatment centre at **Croid**, Vuelta de Obligado 1551 (Belgrano), T4781 9037, www.croid.com.ar. **Dental Argentina**, Laprida 1621, p 2 B, T4828 0821, www.dental-argentina.com.ar.

Useful addresses

Migraciones: (Immigration), Antártida Argentina 1355, edif 4, T4317 0234, www.migraciones.gov.ar, 0800-1400. **Central Police Station**: Moreno 1550, Virrey Cevallos 362, T4346 5700 (emergency, T101 or 911 from any phone, free). **Aves Argentinas/AOP** (a BirdLife International partner), Matheu 1246, T4943 7216, www. avesargentinas.org.ar. For information on birdwatching and specialist tours, good library, open Mon-Fri 1030-1330, 1430-2030 (closed Jan). Student organizations: **Asatej**: Helpful Argentine Youth and Student Travel Organization, runs a Student Flight Centre, Florida 835, p 3, oficina 320, T4114 7528, www. asatej.com, Mon-Fri 1000-1900 (with many branches in BA and around the country). Booking for flights (student discounts) including cheap 1-way flights (long waiting lists), hotels and travel; information for all South America, notice board for travellers, ISIC cards sold (giving extensive discounts; Argentine ISIC guide available here), English and French spoken. Cheap fares also at **TIJE**, San Martín 601, T5272 8480 or branches at Av Santa Fe 898, T5272 8450, and elsewhere in the city, Argentina, Uruguay and Chile, www. tije.com. **YMCA**: (Central), Reconquista 439, T4311 4785, www.ymca.org.ar. **YWCA**: Humberto 1º 2360, T4941 3776, www.ywca.org.ar.

Contents

Footnotes

Index

Notes

About the author

Anna Maria Espsäter is a London-based Swedish travel and food writer. She's written some 350 features for a variety of publications in the UK, US, Australia, the Netherlands and Sweden, as well as authored, co-authored or contributed to over a dozen books. With 90 countries visited to date, she occasionally considers retiring at 100. Latin America and Scandinavia are her favourite parts of the world.

Acknowledgements

Anna Maria would like to thank: Nicolás Kugler for the Buenos Aires chapter. Ben Box, Patrick Dawson, Felicity Laughton and everyone at Footprint; Bryony Addis-Jones and Caroline Maughan for support and inspiration. In Uruguay: Diana Valente; Steven Chew; Ines Gamarra from Branding Latin America; VIK Retreats; Paola Pirelli from Lares tours; Cecilia Ribó from Posada Valizas.

Titles available in the Footprint *Focus* range

Latin America	UK RRP	US RRP
Bahia & Salvador	£7.99	$11.95
Brazilian Amazon	£7.99	$11.95
Brazilian Pantanal	£6.99	$9.95
Buenos Aires & Pampas	£7.99	$11.95
Cartagena & Caribbean Coast	£7.99	$11.95
Costa Rica	£8.99	$12.95
Cuzco, La Paz & Lake Titicaca	£8.99	$12.95
El Salvador	£5.99	$8.95
Guadalajara & Pacific Coast	£6.99	$9.95
Guatemala	£8.99	$12.95
Guyana, Guyane & Suriname	£5.99	$8.95
Havana	£6.99	$9.95
Honduras	£7.99	$11.95
Nicaragua	£7.99	$11.95
Northeast Argentina & Uruguay	£8.99	$12.95
Paraguay	£5.99	$8.95
Quito & Galápagos Islands	£7.99	$11.95
Recife & Northeast Brazil	£7.99	$11.95
Rio de Janeiro	£8.99	$12.95
São Paulo	£5.99	$8.95
Uruguay	£6.99	$9.95
Venezuela	£8.99	$12.95
Yucatán Peninsula	£6.99	$9.95

Asia	UK RRP	US RRP
Angkor Wat	£5.99	$8.95
Bali & Lombok	£8.99	$12.95
Chennai & Tamil Nadu	£8.99	$12.95
Chiang Mai & Northern Thailand	£7.99	$11.95
Goa	£6.99	$9.95
Gulf of Thailand	£8.99	$12.95
Hanoi & Northern Vietnam	£8.99	$12.95
Ho Chi Minh City & Mekong Delta	£7.99	$11.95
Java	£7.99	$11.95
Kerala	£7.99	$11.95
Kolkata & West Bengal	£5.99	$8.95
Mumbai & Gujarat	£8.99	$12.95

Africa & Middle East	UK RRP	US RRP
Beirut	£6.99	$9.95
Cairo & Nile Delta	£8.99	$12.95
Damascus	£5.99	$8.95
Durban & KwaZulu Natal	£8.99	$12.95
Fès & Northern Morocco	£8.99	$12.95
Jerusalem	£8.99	$12.95
Johannesburg & Kruger National Park	£7.99	$11.95
Kenya's Beaches	£8.99	$12.95
Kilimanjaro & Northern Tanzania	£8.99	$12.95
Luxor to Aswan	£8.99	$12.95
Nairobi & Rift Valley	£7.99	$11.95
Red Sea & Sinai	£7.99	$11.95
Zanzibar & Pemba	£7.99	$11.95

Europe	UK RRP	US RRP
Bilbao & Basque Region	£6.99	$9.95
Brittany West Coast	£7.99	$11.95
Cádiz & Costa de la Luz	£6.99	$9.95
Granada & Sierra Nevada	£6.99	$9.95
Languedoc: Carcassonne to Montpellier	£7.99	$11.95
Málaga	£5.99	$8.95
Marseille & Western Provence	£7.99	$11.95
Orkney & Shetland Islands	£5.99	$8.95
Santander & Picos de Europa	£7.99	$11.95
Sardinia: Alghero & the North	£7.99	$11.95
Sardinia: Cagliari & the South	£7.99	$11.95
Seville	£5.99	$8.95
Sicily: Palermo & the Northwest	£7.99	$11.95
Sicily: Catania & the Southeast	£7.99	$11.95
Siena & Southern Tuscany	£7.99	$11.95
Sorrento, Capri & Amalfi Coast	£6.99	$9.95
Skye & Outer Hebrides	£6.99	$9.95
Verona & Lake Garda	£7.99	$11.95

North America	UK RRP	US RRP
Vancouver & Rockies	£8.99	$12.95

Australasia	UK RRP	US RRP
Brisbane & Queensland	£8.99	$12.95
Perth	£7.99	$11.95

For the latest books, e-books and a wealth of travel information, visit us at:
www.footprinttravelguides.com

Join us on facebook for the latest travel news, product releases, offers and amazing competitions:
www.facebook.com/footprintbooks.